"I've got some interesting news for you, Longarm— you're fired!"

Longarm took the cheroot out of his mouth and looked closely at Vail. He was waiting for the man's face to break into a grin. It didn't.

"Okay. I'll bite. What's up?"

"Simple. If you're no longer a deputy U.S. marshal, you can go after a son of a bitch this government would like to see stopped—even if the bastard is beyond our jurisdiction."

"Who is this son of a bitch, Billy?"

"Name's James B. Hook. A hired killer. No one ever sees him, but he never misses. If you get him, there just might be a bonus in it for you, a sizable one.

"If anything goes wrong, no one in Washington knows who you are."

TABOR EVANS

LONGARM

AND THE BLOOD BOUNTY

JOVE BOOKS, NEW YORK

LONGARM AND THE BLOOD BOUNTY

A Jove Book/published by arrangement with
the author

PRINTING HISTORY
Jove edition/August 1988

ISBN: 0-515-09682-2

Jove Books are published by The Berkley Publishing Group,
200 Madison Avenue, New York, New York 10016.
The name "JOVE" and the "J" logo
are trademarks belonging to Jove Publications, Inc.

PRINTED IN THE UNITED STATES OF AMERICA

10 9 8 7 6 5 4 3 2 1

Chapter 1

There was a pleased, almost contented smile on Long-arm's face as he strode up Colfax Avenue, heading toward the gleaming dome of the Colorado State House. He had taken more than his usual share away from the poker table the evening before, after which he had spent the night with a lovely young widow of his acquaintance who had journeyed in from the prairie for a visit. As she had put it, women were a lot like men. They too had to get their ashes hauled once in a while.

As usual, she had wanted him to put behind him his present employment and consider instead a career as her foreman on a ranch half the size of Texas. He was willing to humor her—she was too pretty not to—but such a proposition did not appeal to him at the moment, despite the amorous side benefits he could count on as this fiery young widow's foreman. Someday he might have

1

to consider such an option. He couldn't spend the rest of his days chasing no-accounts—and he sure as hell did not want to end up like poor Billy Vail, turning to suet behind a desk.

Right now he had no worry on that score. He was still on the comfortable side of forty, a vigorous, striking figure as he strode on through the bright morning air of the Mile High City. The raw sun and cutting winds he had ridden through since coming west from West-by-God-Virginia had cured his rawboned features to a saddle-leather brown. His eyes were gunmetal blue over high cheekbones, and only the tobacco-leaf shade of his close-cropped hair and his longhorn mustache gave evidence of his Anglo-Saxon heritage. Otherwise, to the casual observer, he could easily have passed for a full-blooded Indian.

His snuff-brown Stetson was tilted slightly forward, the hat's crown telescoped in the Colorado rider's fashion. Over his vest he wore a brown frock coat that matched his brown tweed pants, which clung to his lean frame snugly. They had been purchased purposely small, since Longarm knew the dangers of a sweat-soaked fold of cloth or leather between a rider and his mount. For a similar reason, his low-heeled cavalry stovepipes had also been purchased a size too small, soaked overnight, then put on wet. As they were broken in, they molded to his feet. Since he spent as much time on foot as he did astride a horse, he could run in these boots with surprising speed for a man his size.

On his left side under his frock coat he carried a Colt Model T .44-40 in a cross-draw rig fashioned of waxed and heat-hardened leather. And in his right vest pocket, acting as his watch fob, rested a double-barreled .44

derringer. For a small gun it packed a considerable wallop and had proven its worth on more than one occasion.

Longarm increased his pace as he neared his place of employment, his tall figure cutting through the morning crowd like a shark's fin cutting through water. No one tested his resolve as he approached them, content to duck aside as the intent man in the brown tweed frock coat swept toward them. Reaching the federal courthouse, he mounted the steps, pushed through the crowded first-floor lobby and climbed the marble staircase. Striding down a short hall, he came to a door on which gold-leaf lettering proclaimed: UNITED STATES MARSHAL, FIRST DISTRICT COURT OF COLORADO. Pushing through it, he skirted a young clerk pounding on a ponderous-looking typewriting machine, knocked once on Billy Vail's office door, and strode in.

"That's right," said Vail, looking up from his desk. "Just walk right in. I could've been in conference with a young filly. But you wouldn't care."

Longarm slumped into Vail's morocco-leather armchair. "Hell, chief, I wouldn't mind. I'd cheer you on."

"At my age, you should," Vail said gruffly. Then he looked unhappily back at his cluttered desk. "I'll be with you in a minute. Some damned bureaucrat in Washington will pee in his pants if I don't get this here report off to him right now. Today."

Longarm lit up a cheroot and leaned back in his chair and watched his harried superior clawing through the mountain of paperwork that got shoveled onto him day after day. In his salad days Marshal Billy Vail had shot it out with Comanche, assorted owlhoots, and to hear him tell it, half the *bandidos* in Mexico. But now his bar-bered jowls were soft, almost pink, as if advancing age were turning him back into an infant.

At last, with a deep, troubled sigh, Billy Vail pushed aside the papers on the blotter in front of him and ran his pudgy hand over his balding pate. Blinking owlishly at Longarm, he said, "I've got some interesting news for you, Longarm."

Longarm puffed casually. "I'm listening, Billy."

"You're fired."

Longarm took the cheroot out of his mouth and looked closely at Vail. He was waiting for the man's face to break into a grin. It didn't. "What's the matter, Billy? You constipated or something?"

"I'm serious, Mr. Long. You are fired. As of"—Vail glanced at the banjo clock on his wall—"eight-fifteen today. I've already got the ball rolling by complaining like hell about the way you come bargin' in here without a by-your-leave and can never seem to make it to work on time."

"Okay. I'll bite. What's up?"

"Simple. If you're no longer a deputy U.S. marshal, you can go after a son of a bitch this government would like to see stopped—even if the bastard is beyond our jurisdiction."

"Who is this son of a bitch, Billy?"

"Name's James B. Hook. A hired killer. Likes to dress up in black and knows how to handle the tools of his trade. He goes to the highest bidder, from all we can gather. No one ever sees him, but he never misses. He stays out of sight for long periods, then he pops up in some town, makes friends and settles in. That's when the killings begin. When his job is done, he vanishes."

"How far does he range?"

4

"There's been reports that he's accepted assignments as far east as Buffalo. But that don't matter. He favors it out here. Plenty of territory for him to get lost in. I wouldn't be surprised if he's a rich man by now. Probably owns a fine horse ranch somewhere. I wouldn't put it past the bastard."

"And you want this child to bring him in without a warrant. And to do that he's going to get his ass fired."

"I admit it sounds crazy at first crack, Longarm."

"You're damn right it sounds crazy. At first and second crack. Leave me out of it, Billy. Send Wallace. He's gettin' itchy feet again."

"No, not Wallace. I want my *best* man on this, Longarm."

"I'll tell Wallace you said that. It'll give him all kinds of confidence the next time you send him out to get his butt shot off."

"Sweet suffering Jesus! Don't tell him that! What the hell's got into you, Custis? You used to be a nicy guy."

Longarm stretched out his long legs and crossed his ankles. "I played poker last night, Billy. There's fresh bills in my kick. It does things for a man."

"All right, now listen. If you get this son of a bitch —and we aren't telling you how, exactly—there just might be a bonus in it for you, a sizable one. Washington wants this guy and they'll back me in this. Thing is, you can't use your shield. After you get officially fired, you'll be just another citizen."

"And as naked as a plucked chicken on a fox farm."

"I mean if anything goes wrong, no one in Washington knows who you are. And if you do get a department citation and bonus for doing this, no one in the marshal's office will admit to it."

5

"So I can't mention it when I go for a promotion."

"Aw, hell, Longarm. Since when're you looking for a desk job? Man like you'd go to seed quicker'n me. Now that widow you was seen with last night might be just the ticket to keep you young. With that bonus, you might be able to buy into her spread."

"All right, Billy. What leads have you got? This fellow Hook must have surfaced again, I gather."

Vail did not hide his relief as he pushed a file envelope across his desk toward Longarm. "Here's the file on Hook. His description's in there, along with a list of his victims. There aren't any sketches of the man. What we do know is what I told you—that and the fact that he's just arrived in Sand Hills, New Mexico. No one's dead yet, but if he sticks to his usual plan of operation, bodies will begin to pile up."

"How do I get there?"

"You can't make it there by train, not all the way. You'll have to take a stage from Socorro."

Longarm uncrossed his legs and sat up in the chair. "When do I leave?"

Vail tapped the file. "Your tickets and a bank draft for five hundred dollars are in there, along with a letter of dismissal. Disrespect and insubordination are the grounds. Don't read it. You'll only get your feathers ruffled. But it's just in there to cover our asses."

Longarm chuckled. The old buzzard had known all along he'd go for this crazy assignment. "Seems to me you were taking me a mite for granted, Billy."

"Maybe. But just a mite. Hell, you ain't a man to pull back from a tough assignment. And stayin' in cheap hotels to bring in smelly no-accounts ain't your style, Custis. Besides, this here undercover work is real glamorous. Look at how much fun the Pinkertons have —and don't forget that bonus."

Longarm took the file from the desk and stood up. With a casual wave he opened the door to Vail's office and left. But Vail called out to him before he could close the door. Longarm ducked his head back into the office.

"Don't sit with your back to any doors, Custis. This man's a killer."

"Just have that bonus waiting, Billy."

Longarm closed the door and strode from the office, the file under his arm. He figured he'd have plenty of time to go over it on the train. It promised to make interesting reading.

Hidden in the shadows atop the canyon wall, a man dressed in black was resting with his back to a huge boulder. He was slowly, contentedly smoking a cigar. His face was gaunt, hawklike, with dark, hooded eyes. He was as spare as a rake handle, not an ounce of extra tallow on his tall frame. He could have been anywhere from thirty to forty-five. But age seemed to have passed him by—that is, the process of aging had. It was as if he had never been younger and would never get older, a man timeless.

He wore the clothes of an undertaker, or a professional gambler. And in a way, he was both. He favored a black, low-crowned, flat-brimmed hat, black frock coat, white broadcloth shirt with a black string tie knotted at his neck. His vest was gray, of a silken texture, and he kept it neatly buttoned at all times. Tight-fitting black trousers, which were fashionable now, and hand-tooled boots that would have cost a cowpuncher a year's wages, completed his somber garb.

There was a quiet air of competence about the man, as if he had found a means of expressing himself completely through his profession. He was a killer and a stalker of men, an employment that afforded him a good living, making his remuneration during his days as a buffalo and Indian hunter seem pitiful by comparison.

Despite the nature of his profession, there was no handgun riding his hip. There was only the Winchester rifle leaning against the boulder beside him and a large, murderous bowie knife in a sheath fitted to his belt, tucked away in the small of his back.

As he took a drag on his cigar he paused, his eyes narrowing. A thin cloud of dust had just become visible. His habitual, guarded expression did not change, but he held the cigar smoke in his lungs for an instant or two as he peered into the distance. When he was certain his eyes had not been playing tricks on him, he slowly expelled the smoke, dropped the cigar stub, and ground it into the dust at his feet. Then he picked up his rifle and levered a fresh cartridge into the firing chamber with a smooth, infinitely casual movement. Allowing the tension to build up inside him to the proper pitch, he waited for the stage to get closer.

The cloud of dust grew larger. Before long the stagecoach, drawn by a team of four horses, began to take shape. Hook walked forward to the edge of the cliff face and stretched himself out on the cool slate surface, resting the barrel of the rifle in a notch between two rocks. Cradling the stock between his cheek and shoulder, he lined up his sights on the rocking coach.

It was one of the line's new stagecoaches, Hook noted, pleased—its black and red, lacquered surface gleaming, its bright yellow wheels throwing back sun-

8

light, a thick rooster tail of dust following behind. There was someone on the driver's box beside Tomlinson, Hook noted, but this made no difference at all to him as he waited for the stage to get closer.

Tomlinson was keeping the stage close to the center of the canyon, which was wise, since the cliff faces on either side had been crumbling away for hundreds of years, resulting in massive piles of rocks and fallen boulders along the base of each cliff.

Still following the approaching stage with his sights locked on to it, he slid his finger across the trigger and then shifted his aim to the horses. Carefully, he gauged the distance, the speed of the horses, the faint breeze. The stage was almost directly across from him now. He could hear clearly the hooves pounding and the rattling of the stay chains, the creaking of the wheels and leather slings under the coach. Hook drew a shallow breath, held it for a brief moment, then gently squeezed the trigger.

The crack of the rifle echoed sharply as the near lead horse went down in its traces, dragging the other three horses with it and bringing the stagecoach to a skidding, jolting halt. By then Hook had already jacked a fresh load into his firing chamber and shifted his aim to the rear-wheel horse. Coolly, he squeezed off his second shot, catching the animal in the head, toppling it over against its wildly plunging teammate.

Levering another cartridge into the rifle's chamber, Hook watched as the terrified passengers spilled frantically out of the coach while Tomlinson and the fellow up on the box beside him dropped swiftly to the ground. Tomlinson was carrying a rifle, and the other one had taken out a handgun. Hook chuckled meanly. A fat lot of good a side arm would do.

As the passengers scuttled around behind the stage to gain cover, Tomlinson and his companion raced across the canyon floor toward Hook. From that distance there was no way they could hit him, and he felt perfectly safe as he watched them. Neither man was firing wildly or injudiciously, and this impressed Hook. As he had long suspected, Tomlinson was no tenderfoot when it came to gunplay. Who his tall friend was, however, Hook had no idea; probably just some dude with a new six-gun who had asked Tomlinson for the privilege of riding up on the box beside the driver. Hook watched patiently as the two men scrambled over the rocky canyon floor, heading for the base of the cliff beneath Hook, evidently hoping to work their way up the steep slope to his position.

Hook waited grimly, pleased. It was all going as he had planned—or as Bull Denton had told him it would. Both of the men were near the base of the cliff by this time. Tomlinson's heavy figure—his short, thick legs propelling him with surprising speed over the uneven ground—made an excellent target as he kept just a little ahead of the tall fellow with him.

Again tucking his rifle into the crook in his shoulder, Hook followed Tomlinson in his sights, led him a bit, adjusted for the fact that he was aiming down from a height and at a tricky angle—and fired. The bullet kicked up a geyser of dirt just behind the running man. Continuing to follow him with his rifle sights, Hook made a finer allowance for the angle, led the runner by a fraction more—and fired again.

The bullet hit Tomlinson in the side and bowled him

off his feet. He hit the ground on one shoulder, rolled completely over, and immediately began dragging himself toward the nearest boulder. Hook glanced to the spot where he'd last seen the other one, the tall fellow in the dark-brown frock coat. For a man with boots, he seemed to have been moving pretty damn fast.

Whoever the hell he was, he was no longer in sight. That meant he'd reached the rocks directly below and was on his way up. A cheeky son of a bitch, Hook realized, and decided he had better revise his estimate of the man's skill and courage.

Hook looked back at Tomlinson. He was still alive, still crawling toward the boulder for cover. Back in the middle of the canyon the six or seven passengers were cowering behind the stage while the two uninjured horses were trying vainly to free themselves from the dead horses attached to them by the tangled harness rig. As a warning to the passengers, to make sure they kept out of this, Hook raised his rifle and sent two bullets into the side of the new stagecoach, punching holes through the woodwork and tearing up the leather seats inside. He chuckled softly as he saw some of the passengers behind the coach break for the far side of the canyon.

This further bit of intimidation completed, Hook coolly thumbed fresh cartridges into the rifle's magazine, loading it with a swift, practiced ease that had no appearance of haste. He was, in fact, looking forward to the upcoming duel.

The reloading completed, he moved off the ledge in a crouch, carrying his rifle in both hands. The rear of the cliff was as much of a ruin as the front, tumbling down into a maze of boulders, broken sandstone pillars,

11

and twisting ravines. It was somewhere down there in that tangled badland that he had tethered his horse. But he was no fool, and before going for it, he decided he would check first on the tall fellow with the six-gun coming at him from the other side. Moving silently onto a massive shoulder of rock, he flattened himself onto it and peered over its edge at the long gully below him, up which he assumed the tall fellow would be climbing.

But the gully was empty.

Hook stiffened. Then he looked around quickly. Where the hell was the son of a bitch? Hook cursed himself for underestimating him. The gully was the only way up to the spot from which Hook had been firing. This meant that the fellow with the Colt was not coming directly for him. Instead, he was swinging around behind the cliff, going for Hook's mount, knowing that it must be on the back slope somewhere; it could never have been ridden up onto this cliff. Clever. At this moment, then, this tall drink of water was doing his best to get between Hook and his waiting horse.

So be it, then. Despite Denton's promises, White Pine Junction had been getting pretty dull. This little exercise out in the bright mountain air should go far to liven things up.

Hook pushed himself back off the boulder, turned, and began to work himself down the treacherous slope.

Longarm sat back on his heels, an unlit cheroot in his mouth, studying the terrain below him. He was certain that somewhere down in that tangle of ravines and boulders the sniper had tethered his horse. He turned his head and squinted upward, searching the rimrocks for some sign of the sniper who had stopped the stage with those well-aimed shots. It had not been more than a few minutes since the last crackling shot had brought down the driver. Whoever was up there could not have gotten away yet.

He kept his head cocked as he listened for the sound of sand and gravel rattling loose and tumbling down over rock faces, starting small avalanches. It would be almost impossible for anyone to come down off that disintegrating shelf of rock without sending some loose gravel down ahead of him.

But though Longarm watched and listened intently for some time, there was no sound of tumbling rocks, no sign at all of the sniper, and he turned his attention back to the badlands below him. The sniper's horse had to be close by, since the sniper would not have wanted to go any distance for his mount after stopping the stage. After a keen appraisal of the tortured gullies and rock forms below, he settled on two possible sites where a horse could be hidden. Directly below him was a cluster of boulders. More than one horse could be in there without Longarm being able to see it. Off to the right was the entrance to a deep ravine. A horse could have been taken in and tethered there. But there was a heavy growth of bunchgrass and mesquite in the ravine's mouth, and from this distance Longarm could see that none of it had been trampled.

Longarm decided to check the boulders below him first. Looking back up at the rimrocks, he made a long, careful study of them. He saw no movement. Nothing at all. He turned back around and threaded his way down through the rock formations, following a circuitous route that would give him cover all the way to the boulders below. He took each step with fine-honed caution so as not to dislodge any of the loose shale. As he moved he constantly looked around and above him, searching for any sign of the sniper.

Finally he reached a spot where he could see in among the boulders. For a time he studied the shadows they cast, looking for the contours of a horse's head or hind end. He saw nothing. There was no horse in there. Then he looked again at the mouth of the ravine he had discounted earlier. He was a good deal closer to it now. What he had decided from above still held true. There was absolutely no sign at all that a horse had been led in there. The ravine fairly howled at him that it was empty of horseflesh.

Longarm looked up again at the rimrocks, searching for sign of the sniper. He was thinking of Tomlinson. The owner of the stage line was shot and down, hiding behind a boulder on the other side of this rock formation. Longarm didn't like leaving him like that.

There was no sign of the sniper. It was as if he had taken flight from that ledge on wings, but Longarm's narrowed eyes kept searching, hoping for a sign, any sign at all, a tail of gravel sifting down, the glint of sunlight on metal.

But there was nothing.

Which meant one of two possibilities: the sniper was still up there, well hidden, waiting for a chance to pick off Longarm; or else he had somehow managed to work himself down, despite Longarm's surveillance, and was already on his way to his horse.

Below Longarm was a narrow gully that led around the field or boulders. He dropped quickly to it and found the gully to be shallower than he had expected, about knee deep. He stretched himself out on the ground

14

and inched along the gully, using his elbows and knees, his body raised a scant inch off the bottom and the Colt held in front of him in his right hand. The gully made a right-hand twist around the nearest boulder. Longarm inched around it, went straight ahead for a few yards, then made another sharp turn.

As soon as he started to make the turn, a rifle blasted at him from a position less than a hundred yards behind him.

Chapter 2

The bullet snicked past the crown of Longarm's hat, then ricocheted off the face of a boulder ahead of him.

Longarm dropped flat, pressing himself down into the gully as far as he could go. The unseen rifle cracked again. A lead slug slapped the rim of the gully just ahead of him and glanced away. Longarm kept his head down, cursing, not moving a muscle. As long as he kept down, he was safe. Evidently the sniper could not see him from where he was shooting—otherwise, neither of those bullets would have missed.

Seconds dragged by without another shot, or sounds of any kind that would indicate to Longarm the sniper's exact location. Longarm's mind was racing meanwhile. The sniper had been firing not at him, but at whatever dust his progress through the gully had raised. His fire then was simply an attempt to keep him pinned.

Longarm rolled over onto his back, the .44 held out in front of him, ready in case the sniper's head popped into view. It didn't. All Longarm could see were jagged rock forms, the cliff side rising behind them, and sky. Turning back around, Longarm began to move as swiftly as he could along the gully. If the son of a bitch had been attempting to keep him from going in this direction, there must be a damned good reason for doing so.

Hook had been waiting patiently, squatting out of sight of the gully in the protection of a jumble of small boulders halfway down the slope. Now, his dark, hooded eyes narrowed. The man in the gully was moving away from him once again. This he could tell from the barely visible stirring of dust he raised as he inched along. Hook continued to watch until he saw the faint dust cloud reach a rock spur at the far end of the gully. There it stopped.

Hook's gaunt, leathery face relaxed a bit. The place the fellow had chosen to hole up in was a good one if his intent was to ambush Hook on his way to his horse. But only if Hook's horse were tethered in the ground pocket in that direction. But it was not. It was inside the ravine at the other end of the slope.

Hook raised up a little and turned away, threading off through the rock formations toward the ravine. As he moved, he used every bit of cover he could find, keeping well down out of sight, his finger still resting lightly across his rifle's trigger. When he reached to within a hundred yards of the ravine's entrance he stopped, turned, and surveyed the maze of rock between him and the gully, looking for a sign that the man he had left hunkered down in the gully might have left it by now and be moving toward him. He saw no dust, no movement, nothing to indicate that he had left the gully.

He turned back and studied the stretch of open ground that still lay between him and the entrance to the ravine. Hook had ridden his horse into it from the other end, which could not be seen from here. And he would ride it out the same way. But he had to enter from this end, and to do that he would have to cross that open stretch with little cover; and no matter how fast he moved, there would be close to a minute when that son of a bitch behind him could race out of the gully and bring his side arm within range of him.

Hood studied the ravine wall and made his decision. Keeping in a low crouch, he followed a circuitous route through the fallen rock and gullies at the base of the ravine until he came to a narrow game trail and followed it swiftly up to the top of the ravine. Taking off his hat and lifting his head cautiously, he peered back and down along the path he had taken. He could see the mouth of the gully where the man should still be crouching.

The gully was empty.

Hook's glance swept over the tortured landscape below him. Where was the son of a bitch? He stepped quickly to the edge of the ravine and was about to drop into it when a six-gun barked from less than fifty yards away. The bullet thudded into the stock of his rifle, slamming the stock into his chest with crushing force. He gasped, and as the rifle spilled from his numbed hand, he toppled straight down into the mesquite-choked ravine.

• • •

19

Hunkered down under a shale overhang some fifty yards from the ravine, Longarm had been watching the ravine entrance closely for the past minute or two. He had scuttled out of the gully once he realized that nothing was to be gained by staying there. He was about to give up on the ravine and head back to see about Tomlinson when he caught the blur of movement higher up. He stood quickly. The new angle gave him a clear look at the black-garbed sniper peering down into the ravine. He lifted his .44, aimed carefully, and fired. The sniper appeared to duck out of sight. Longarm cursed. At that distance, he should have at least winged him.

He raced around behind the ravine, found the trail the sniper must have used, and scrambled up it, moving as fast as he could on the treacherous, shale-littered slope. He made enough racket during his climb to alert half the southwest, but he kept going nevertheless, and reaching a spot on the trail a few feet above the top of the ravine, he leaped onto its lip and crouched down behind a crumbling sandstone pillar.

The sniper's rifle was lying on the ground on the other side of the pillar, near the edge of the ravine. He could see the stock clearly. His bullet was embedded deep in it. Skirting the pillar, Longarm dropped to his knees and peered into the ravine.

He saw the mesquite brush carpeting its floor. And that was all. The sniper was gone. Even as Longarm straightened up, looking for a way down, he heard the distant pound of hooves coming from the other end of the ravine. In a moment the only sound was that of the wind whispering mournfully through the rock formations all about him.

* * *

The wounded stage driver—owner of the Sand Hills Mountain Line—was slumped on the ground, leaning against the rock behind which he had taken cover. As Longarm got closer, he could see how ashen the man's face was as he squeezed his eyes shut against the pain. Both hands were pressing a wadded bandanna to his right side. The wad and the area of bullet-torn shirt around it were soaked with blood. The man's breathing was short, rasping unpleasantly through his clenched teeth.

And not a single one of the passengers had come across the canyon floor to see to him.

Back at the express office in Socorro, Longarm had introduced himself to the owner of the stage line as Jud Drake and let it be known that he had some money and might be interested in building a hotel in Sand Hills. He had heard of the town's sudden prosperity, he told Tomlinson, referring to the recent reopening of a nearby silver mine. He kept all this in mind now as he reached the stage driver.

"You don't look so good, Tomlinson," Longarm said, getting down on one knee beside the man. "How do you feel?"

"Did you get the bastard?"

"Nope."

"Didn't think you would. Should've come back for my rifle."

"That's right, I should have. Wasn't thinking, I guess."

"Forget it. You ain't no gunslick, that's for sure."

Longarm pushed away the blood-soaked bandanna to examine the man's wound. The bullet had ranged along one of his ribs, digging a nasty-looking trench from

21

under his armpit to below the nipple. Longarm sat back on his heels and looked with some relief at Tomlinson.

"Could've been worse," he told the man. "A lot worse. The slug tore a lot of flesh out of you and went on its way. You won't even have to dig it out."

"I think it cracked one of my ribs."

Longarm nodded briefly. "Could be. Let's go."

Longarm got Tomlinson's left arm around his shoulders and hauled him to his feet. He was as heavy as a potato sack full of stones, but he was able to put enough weight on his own legs to help Longarm get him to the stage. As they approached it, the three other men—two of them whiskey drummers, the third a gambler—stepped out from behind the stage. The two women passengers kept close beside the gambler. They were both young and saucy-looking, if a little sweaty and nervous from their ordeal.

Ignoring the passengers, Longarm dumped Tomlinson on the rear coach seat, unfolded the jump seat, and put Tomlinson's legs up onto it to get him in a reclining position. Rummaging in the front boot for a full canteen and an old cotton shirt, he cleaned the wound and then tore up the shirt and made a tight bandage out of it to staunch the bleeding. When he was finished, Tomlinson lay cautiously back against the rear seat, his eyes closed, and seemed to be breathing a little easier.

Then Longarm stepped down out of the coach and approached the three men. "If you want to walk, you can. If you want to ride, get those dead horses out of the traces and hitch up the other two."

"Who's goin' to drive the coach?" one of the drummers asked.

Longarm hesitated for only a second. "I will."

22

The men appeared to hesitate. Longarm smiled. "I meant it, you bastards. You let Tomlinson bleed out there in the hot sun while you hid behind these ladies' skirts. Now it's time you did some work."

"Or what?" said the gambler.

Without a word, Longarm turned to face the gambler. He had just lost the man he had come a long way to get, and this gambler in front of him would be a nice consolation prize. The gambler shifted uncomfortably under Longarm's cold, waiting gaze.

"Just askin', friend."

"Then stop asking and get busy."

While the three men set to work hauling away the dead horses, Longarm went back for Tomlinson's rifle and the one left by the sniper. He tossed them into the front boot next to his gear, then helped the men with the two horses. One of them was so skittish, it took two of the men to hold it while a third backed him into the traces and hitched him up.

At last they were ready to go. Longarm waited for the passengers to climb in, mounted the driver's box, took up the ribbons, released the brake, and with a shout at the two horses, headed out of the canyon for Sand Hills.

About three in the afternoon, two hours late, Longarm brought the stage into Sand Hills, a dusty sprawl of adobe and freshly constructed wooden-frame buildings set in the notch of a pass that cut through the mountain range. The squat adobe jailhouse, the express office, a hotel, a general store, saloons, and a grain mill fronted a cramped plaza.

Almost before Longarm pulled the stage to a halt in

front of the express office, the passengers pushed open the doors and spilled hastily out. Clutching their sample cases, the two drummers made for a nearby saloon, while the gambler swung up onto the carriage rack on top of the stage and began tossing down his and the ladies' luggage.

Longarm looped the ribbons around the brake handle and climbed down. He had had no gloves to protect his hands and they were raw from handling the reins. He took off his hat and slammed it against his thighs to rid the brim of the dust clinging to it. He was looking forward to some Maryland rye to clean off his tonsils, but first things first. He walked over to the coach's side door and pulled it open.

Tomlinson, his face as gray as the alkali dust on Longarm's frock coat, was trying to sit up.

Looking after the fleeing passengers, he rasped, "I never saw rats desert a sinking ship so fast in my life."

Glancing over his shoulder, Longarm saw the gambler escorting his two lady friends toward a newly constructed frame dwelling farther down the street. The three were moving along at a brisk pace, not one of them taking a look back.

"You know how some people are, Tomlinson. They don't like to get involved."

"Not that bunch, anyway."

Longarm reached in and helped Tomlinson to a sitting position. Taking it very easy, he gently nudged Tomlinson out of the coach, catching him about the shoulders to support him.

"Where's Jane?" Tomlinson gasped.

"Jane?"

"My daughter. She runs the office."

Even as he spoke, the express office door was flung open. Longarm turned and saw an anxious young lady rush out. Without bothering to use the steps, she jumped off the porch and ran toward the stage. Two stable boys and an old man were hurrying from the horse barns set back in the alley.

"Dad! You've been hurt!" the young lady cried, rushing up to her father. "What happened?"

"Don't get all excited," he told her. "I'm going to live." He looked at Longarm. "Meet my daughter, Drake."

"Howdy, Jane," Longarm said, touching his hat brim lightly. "Your father should be fine. A sniper killed two horses, and your father caught a slug when we went after him. But it didn't hit anything vital, just cracked a rib."

Longarm's words calmed Jane some, but she was still very concerned. She looked at her father searchingly. "It must hurt terribly, Dad. Does it?"

Tomlinson tapped the makeshift bandage Longarm had fashioned and grinned feebly. "It hurts some, but Drake's right," he assured her. "I'll be all right, but I don't think I'm going to be much help around here for a while."

"Never mind about that," she told him fiercely. "We'll be able to hold things together. Don't you let that worry you."

She turned to Longarm. "And thank you, Mr. Drake. Thank you very much. I can see the rest of the passengers weren't much help."

"They were just scared, Jane."

"It's a wonder they didn't trip over the yellow stripe runnin' down their backs. Thanks again."

By this time the two stable boys and the old man, the horse wrangler obviously, arrived at the stage. Longarm stepped back to let Jane take charge. With the aid of the old man and one of the stable boys, she helped her father up the steps and into the express office, while the other stable boy took off flying for the doctor.

A crowd had gathered on the sidewalk to watch. By the time Longarm was ready to head for the saloon, he had to push his way through a formidable throng, every eye peering at him eagerly, hoping for the details on what had happened to the stage and Ben Tomlinson.

As Longarm gained the sidewalk, someone in back yelled, "What happened, mister?"

Longarm knew better than to converse with a crowd or anyone in it. He ignored the question and strode on without pause, shouldering through the batwings into the saloon. He bellied up to the bar and ordered a whiskey when he found the place had no stores of Maryland rye. Lugging his bottle and glass over to a table in back, he slumped into a chair, pushed his hat off his forehead, and poured himself two swift jolts. Downing them, he tipped his chair back against the wall and glared sourly at the crowd of men pushing into the saloon after him.

Silently, they stared at him, waiting for him to say something, while more excited townsmen crowded into the saloon. Longarm said nothing, nursed his drink, and stared back.

"Ain't you gonna tell us what happened, mister?" a short fellow in a derby hat asked. He was stocky and red-faced, and sported a white vest and spats. His voice had a certain authority to it, and the men around him gave him room. Longarm figured he might be the mayor, or the head of the town council.

Longarm looked around for the whiskey drummers. They should have been willing to talk. They could probably manage to cadge quite a few drinks if they played their hands carefully enough. But they seemed to have disappeared. Looking back at the man in the derby, Longarm said nothing. When, after few moments had passed and the man in the derby realized Longarm was not going to tell him a damn thing, he turned and stalked out.

The rest of the crowd, the men muttering and a few casting sullen glances in Longarm's direction, followed his example and pushed out of the saloon. A few stayed behind to belly up to the bar. Longarm took a deep breath and poured his third drink. This one he sipped slowly, letting its warmth work through him. There was still a little alkali dust left on his tonsils, but he had great faith he would eventually get that washed away.

When he did, not too long after, he paid the barkeep for the bottle and walked down the street to the hotel and registered. His room was on the second floor and faced the street. He would have wished for a quieter room, but realized it would probably be best for him to have a view that would keep him in touch with the action below. This promised to be a wide-open town when night fell.

After he inspected the room, he left the hotel to get his gear and see how Tomlinson was doing. As he neared the stage line's office, he saw a burly stage driver climbing up onto the stage's box and take up the ribbons. The bullet holes punched through the coach's side panels by the sniper had not been repaired, but four fresh horses were in the traces, and there were six passengers inside the coach. The Sand Hills Mountain Line was apparently hauling considerable traffic. As Longarm mounted the express office steps, the driver sent his whip crackling over the backs of the horses and the coach lurched forward to resume its run.

Longarm entered the express office. Behind a low fence, a gangling fellow with a green eyeshade was manning a desk.

"I just got off that stage," Longarm told the clerk. "Where's my gear?"

"You Mr. Drake?"

"That's me, all right."

"Come right this way." The clerk pushed open a small gate.

Longarm walked through it and followed the clerk through a door into the warehouse and saw his Winchester, valise, and carpetbag lined up neatly on the loading platform. The sniper's rifle was lying alongside his.

As Longarm started toward his gear, the clerk said, "Miss Jane said if you came for this, she'd like you to stop up and see her."

"Where is she?"

"Upstairs," the clerk said, pointing to a stairway farther down the warehouse. "She and her pa fixed up an apartment on the second floor."

"Much obliged. What's your name, mister?"

"Fred. I'm sure glad you was on hand to help Tommy."

"Tommy?"

"That's what we all call Mr. Tomlinson."

"Would you have someone bring this gear over to my room at the hotel. It's room twenty."

"I'll see to it myself, Mr. Drake."

"I'm much obliged. Take special care of those two rifles."

A moment later Longarm knocked on the apartment door and was let in by Jane Tomlinson. She beamed when she saw him.

"Mr. Drake! Do come in!"

"How's your father?"

"The doctor's with him now."

She closed the door and led him through a living room and into a large bedroom. Tomlinson, in a fresh pair of long johns, was sitting up on the bed, his back leaning against the headboard while the doctor finished knotting an extensive bandage about Tomlinson's ribs. Tomlinson greeted Longarm with a feeble wave. The doctor looked up. He was a thin, fine-looking man with white hair and a neat, well-trimmed goatee.

"You the gent that bandaged up Tommy?"

"I did the best I could, Doc."

"You did just fine. You stopped the bleeding and cleaned out the wound. There wasn't much more you could do, and that was more than sufficient. Doesn't seem to be any infection setting in."

The doc felt Tomlinson's forehead, then took his pulse while observing Tomlinson's heavy, steady breathing. Finally he stood up, closing his black bag.

"Your father's got the constitution of one of his horses," he told Jane.

She smiled, enormously pleased. "Thank God for that."

"It's the whiskey I drink," Tomlinson said.

"More likely," she told him, her face glowing in relief, "it's them old boots you won't ever let me wash out."

Clapping his hat on, the doctor left the room, assuring Jane that he would look in again first thing in the morning. Glancing at Longarm, Jane excused herself and saw the doctor to the door. When she returned a moment later, she went over to her father and took his hand in hers.

"We'll be leaving you now, Dad," she told him gently. "Mr. Drake and I are going to talk."

"Don't mind me," he said, easing himself gingerly down under the covers. "I cold use the rest."

Jane kissed him on the forehead. He patted her hand affectionately and closed his eyes. Following Jane from the room, Longarm glanced back and saw that the exhausted man was already asleep.

Jane led him to the kitchen in the back of the apartment. The stables and corrals were just below, the entire complex taking up a sizable block along the alley running the length of the square. The smell that came from it, compounded of grain, wet hay and horse manure, wasn't all that unpleasant, though Longarm imagined it probably got a little out of control on a few hot, midsummer days.

Jane went straight to the stove, shoving kindling into it and getting a fire going under some coffee, beans, and bacon. Longarm stood in the doorway, leaning against the doorjamb with his arms folded, watching her. She turned her head and flashed a quick smile at him.

"This won't take long. I figured you'd be hungry."

"Thanks. I am."

Smaller than Longarm by half a foot, she did not appear short because of her slim, willowy figure. She wore her braided chestnut hair like a crown, and her features, though not pretty, were handsome and strong.

Her nose was straight, nothing cute about it, her expressive mouth mobile and quick to smile. Her lower lip was full and had a ripeness to it that made him want to kiss her. Very much. What stopped him was her somber gray eyes, the serious cast to her face. It was clear she was a thoughtful young lady, far ahead of anyone else her age. Something had happened to make her grow up fast, he figured, and wondered what it was.

She set out a plate, fork, and spoon for him. Producing two cups and saucers from a cupboard over her sink, she put one down beside his plate, and the other across the table from it.

"I asked Dad about you," she said, glancing up. "He said you were thinking of buying a hotel in town. You don't look like a man who goes around buying hotels."

"You mean I don't look like an innkeeper."

"That's what I meant, yes."

"Well, I figure a good hotel ought to have a nice saloon on the first floor and maybe a place to set up a few poker tables, too."

He saw the faint disappointment in her eyes. "You're a gambler."

He stood away from the doorjamb. "I like to play cards. That's a fact."

She looked at him for a long moment, her gray eyes studying him, her expression somber. He could tell she was considering if the fact that he was a gambler should make any difference in how she felt about him. She went back to the stove. Without looking at him, she said, "A man's got a right to find his own way, his own occupation. You helped Dad out there when no one else did, and for that we will both be eternally grateful."

"Don't make too much of it," he said. "I helped your

31

father because I didn't want that sniper to cut me down next."

"I think you protest too much. But it's nice to have a man around who doesn't brag easy."

"You got any idea who that sniper might be?"

"I have. Did you see him when you were after him?"

"I only saw him for a second. He didn't look very bulky."

"He was thin, you mean."

"Yes. Like a blade."

"The man who shot my father and killed those horses is a man called Hook. I'm sure of it."

"Maybe you could tell me about him."

The coffee was ready. Longarm left the doorway and sat down as Jane filled their cups. Then she set down onto the table a heavy jug of cream and an earthen mug containing honey. The two fixed their coffee, stirred it some, and then Jane told how James B. Hook had arrived in town two weeks ago and had taken a room at the hotel. After a few days he had moved into a second-floor room in the back of the barbershop, enabling him to come and go in perfect privacy. Since then he had been like a spook, never seeming to light, yet turning up everywhere. Though everyone knew he was working for Frank Ellison's partner, Bull Denton, he had never been seen in Denton's company.

"Hold it, now," Longarm said, pushing his empty cup forward. "Maybe you better slow down some. Who's Bull Denton and Frank Ellison?"

She poured him some more coffee, then filled his plate with beans and bacon, and sat down with her coffee.

"Frank Ellison and Denton own the biggest spread in

32

this valley," she said. "He's the law here—or rather, they are."

"How come?"

"Since that silver mine reopened about ten miles deeper into the mountains, there's been a flood of small ranchers and nesters into this area."

"I see. And they have been crowding this rancher Ellison."

"Worse than that. They've moved onto his public grazing land, raided his herds for beef—and six months ago, Ellison and his riders overtook a small rancher he caught rustling his cattle. In the shoot-out Ellison was shot out of his saddle. He's now a cripple."

"Did they get the rancher?"

"They did. And there was a trial."

"I think I know what happened. The local ranchers and nesters and townsmen on the jury let the small rancher go."

"Yes," Jane said. "It was a real miscarriage of justice. Ellison came to court on crutches. He could barely climb out of his buggy to enter the courthouse."

"So now he's getting even."

"He let his foreman, Bull Denton, buy into his spread and become a full partner. He has given Denton full rein. And since then, he's been the only law in these parts. There have been no more jury trials. What there's been instead are night riders, and many of the nesters and small ranchers have had to pull out. Either that or get burned out. As I said, Bull Denton—acting for Frank Ellison—is the law here now."

Pushing away his empty plate, Longarm reached for his mug of coffee. "If this man Hook is working for

Bull Denton, why was your stagecoach a target? What's Denton got against you and your father?"

"It's a pure case of greed, Mr. Drake. Since that mine opened, the line's been doing better and better. So far, there's no talk of a rail line coming in here. It would have nowhere to go after it reached the mine, and that leaves us without any competition. It also leaves us with a fine profit. Last month we bought two more stages. So Denton is no longer satisfied with a half interest in Ellison's holdings. He wants us to sell out to him, and we won't."

"Does Ellison know of this?"

"It doesn't matter if he knows or not. Bull Denton can ride a horse, Ellison can't. Since his injury, he's almost a prisoner out there on his ranch."

"So you're pretty sure it was Bull Denton who sent Hook after your father."

Her face flushed. "Mr. Drake, Denton came in here and told Dad and me we needed protection from highwaymen and Indians. He told us that if we didn't have protection, we'd find ourselves losing stages, suffering injuries. We refused, of course—and look what happened!"

"Neat. You sell out to Denton, or you give him all your profits. He wins either way. But what about the law around here?"

"All we've got is the town marshal. Jimmy Hunnicut. A brave enough kid, but just a kid, and scared to death of Bull Denton or anyone else who works for Ellison."

"What about county and federal law?"

Jane wearily brushed back the few strands that had broken through her braided crown. "County sheriff's

34

ninety miles away. He came once, but what could he do? After all, Ellison is one of the biggest cattlemen in this county, and he's tied in with all the other big spreads around. They swing considerable weight in this state. If the sheriff went against them, he'd be out of office fast. And with that cattleman's lobby in Washington, there won't be any federal marshals riding into this town—not to go against a cattleman as powerful as Frank Ellison or his partner, Denton."

"Looks like they have all the cards."

"Yes. I am afraid so."

"So why are you fighting Denton? Why not sell out, make a good profit and go someplace else?"

She looked at him for a moment or two, as if she were deciding whether or not to take offense at the question. Then she spoke up. "Because I'm not running. And neither is Dad. My husband ran out because he didn't have the sand to stay, and I hope I never see him again. This is our stage line, Mr. Drake, and we aim to keep it come hell or high water."

Longarm was impressed. He sat back in his chair and nodded, a ghost of a smile on his face. "Well, then, I think I'd like another cup of coffee, if you don't mind."

With a weary smile, as if apologizing for her sudden vehemence, Jane got up from the table and started for the stove. Before she reached it, there came a sharp knock on her apartment door. She excused herself hurriedly and left the kitchen to answer it, returning a moment later, her face white.

"You want to see what we've been talking about, Mr. Drake?"

Longarm got up hastily. "What do you mean?"

"Bull Denton's about to lynch a man. The whole town's gathering to watch."

"You mean to stop him."

"I mean to *watch!*"

She turned and hurried from the kitchen, Longarm following quickly after her.

Chapter 3

Jane and Longarm came to a halt on the express office porch. The townspeople were rapidly filling the plaza in front of the adobe jail, while the ladies of the night were crowding into the heads of the alleys and along the sidewalks in front of their parlor houses. A steady stream of farm wagons and buggies were rattling into town, the nesters and small ranchers jumping down and hurrying across the plaza to join the growing crowd.

Some of the nesters brought their families. The skinny, towheaded kids and the bonneted women, like other members of the crowd, seemed completely taken up by the hectic excitement that hung in the air. It was obvious they had accepted the fact of the lynching and regarded it now as a reasonable excuse for an outing. Peering at them, Longarm caught on their faces a mixture of sick fascination and horror—on others, grim acceptance of the inevitable. Beside them on the porch stood the clerk, still wearing his sleeve guards and green eyeshade. It was he who had alerted Jane, and he too was watching the gruesome proceeding as intently and with as much fascination as anyone in the crowd.

"There's been talk all morning about something like this," Jane told Longarm in a hushed voice, "but I just didn't want to believe it."

"Maybe you better fill me in."

"This morning one of Denton's men insulted Dean Clairborn's wife, and when Dean demanded he apologize to her, he slapped Clairborn's wife to the floor and kicked her. That was too much for Dean. He went after the man with a claw hammer and crushed in his skull."

"I'd say he was justified."

"And a fair jury would agree with you. But I already told you. Frank Ellison is in charge now, and he's made Bull Denton the law in Sand Hills."

Longarm glanced at the small adobe jail where the storekeeper was apparently being held. "Isn't anybody going to stop it?"

"Jimmy Hunnicut might try," she replied. "I hope he doesn't. He'll only get himself killed."

"I see. So now we'll all stand around here and watch a lynching."

"Yes," she said with grim cynicism. "And it will be a lesson to all of us."

Longarm noticed a group of townswomen huddled in a storefront a few doors down. One was crying openly, while those about her did their best to calm her. He nodded with his head at the women.

"Would that be Clairborn's wife over there?"

"It would," Jane said, her voice suddenly hollow.

Out from the Silverado saloon a few blocks farther down strode a man Longarm assumed was Bull Denton. An instant and utter silence fell over the spectators as they watched him pull up for a minute on the saloon porch, then step out onto the dusty edge of the plaza and start toward the jail. He was a big, powerful man with a long thin gash of a mouth and eyes the color of dirty ice. He walked with a driving impatience that projected a smouldering, pent-up contempt for lesser men, as if he had never had to and never would step aside for another human being.

Filing out of the Silverado close behind Denton came four more men. The one closest to Denton had two six-guns laced to his thighs. He was a skinny, pasty-faced thug with mean eyes, and narrow, sloping shoulders. He looked like he'd just skittered out from under a stone. Behind him swaggered a thick-waisted fellow with powerful shoulders and a face that looked as if it had been pounded too often and too long. He was hefting an empty wooden barrel on his right shoulder, and in his left hand he held rope and an already-fashioned hangman's noose. There was sure as hell going to be nothing spontaneous about this lynching, Longarm noted. Bringing up the rear of this grim procession came two nondescript gunslicks, each one cradling a carbine in his arm.

Longarm glanced down at Jane. "The first one's Denton. Right?"

"Yes."

"And who're the other two behind him?"

"Denton's hired gunslicks."

"I figured that. What about the thin one right behind him?"

39

"He's called the Kid."

"He looks mean enough."

She shuddered slightly. "He's already killed two men in town who were foolish enough to challenge him while they were still wearing their guns. He's a vicious, cold-blooded killer."

"What about the one carrying the barrel and the rope?"

"That's Slade Cullen. An ex-prizefighter. He has every man in this town thoroughly bullied. They're loathsome creatures, each of them. Whenever one of them rests his eyes on me, my skin begins to crawl."

As Denton neared the jail, the crowd pressed back out of his way, like waves surging back over a partially submerged rock. Without a single glance at any of them, Denton kept on to the jail, the two hirelings with carbines fanning out to take positions on either side of it. The sound they made when they jacked fresh loads into their firing chambers echoed ominously across the hushed plaza.

Mounting the low porch in front of the jail, Denton paused and glanced back. The Kid was standing in the dust by the porch steps, his hands resting on his holsters. Farther back, Slade Cullen had stopped under an oak tree shading a horse trough and was in the act of climbing the barrel he had set down under it. As Denton waited, Slade tossed his rope over a branch, tied it securely to the noose, and hopped down. Then he turned to Denton and nodded.

The party could now begin.

Denton turned back to the door and pounded on it with his fist. "Hunnicut!" he called through the door. "Open up!"

The loud click of the jailhouse door being unlocked flooded across the plaza, then the door swung open and the town marshal stepped out. He was a thin, wiry redhead with a long, lean, freckled face. Young and frightened, it was clear from the grim set of his face that he was determined to deny Denton his victim. He was holding a sawed-off, double-barreled shotgun, its muzzle pointing straight at Denton's gut.

Denton's eyes went down to the shotgun. Then, without a flicker of reaction, his eyes came up again to bore into Hunnicut's. "I want Clairborn, Jimmy. And I want him now."

"You can't have him, Denton."

"Now, dammit, boy! He killed one of my men!"

"That don't matter, Denton. Clairborn deserves a fair trial."

"That'd be a waste of time. He's guilty. And I'm taking him off your hands."

There was a moment of silence. Then the town marshal spoke. "No," he said, his voice trembling slightly. "And get your hired guns off the street. There's an ordinance in this town, and you agreed to it. Anyone carrying side arms in public will have them taken away."

Denton's laugh was short and brutal. "And since when has anyone, you included, dared to enforce that fool law?"

"Well, I'm enforcing it now."

Longarm could see the rivulets of sweat streaming down the young marshal's face. It was clear that Hunnicut was under a great strain, and was battling not only Denton's gunslicks but himself as well. Longarm wondered how much longer the young man could hold out.

"Boy," Denton said softly, "you better drop that shotgun and get out of my way. And I want you to do it *right now.*"

Longarm saw the muscle on the hinge of Hunnicut's jaws bunch into a tight knot. "You may be fast with that gun of yours, Denton," he said stoutly, "but you ain't faster than my finger on this here trigger."

Denton was amused. "You do that, boy, and a split second later you'll be so full of holes it'll take four men to carry you to your grave."

"You'll go with me, Denton. I'll cut you in half with this buckshot."

"That's right," Denton agreed grimly. "Then we'll *both* be dead. It's your decision, boy. So make it. But before you do, look around."

Denton stepped a little to one side and Longarm saw Hunnicut's eyes sweep the crowded plaza, taking in the pale, eager faces waiting for blood, then resting for a moment on the tight knot of women in front of the store —undoubtedly aware that one of them was Clairborn's wife. His eyes dropped then to the Kid's waiting, crouched figure, his pale hands hanging like dead flowers alongside his holsters. Then Hunnicut glanced at the two riflemen on either side of the jail, their cold eyes resting on him—dim, mocking smiles on their jackel-like faces.

And in all that waiting, hushed crowd, there was not a single man willing to step forward and add his voice to the marshal's, or step up beside him to prevent a lynching.

Hunnicut's shoulders sagged, and in that instant Longarm knew it was all over, that Dean Clairborn was doomed. Denton knew this as well. Almost gently he reached up with one hand, and taking hold of the shotgun's twin barrels, pushed them to one side, then pulled the weapon from Hunnicut's grasp. Flinging the shotgun aside, he reached up with one hand and grabbed the town marshal's shirtfront. Hauling him roughly from the doorway, Denton flung him into the dust at his feet.

Beaten, humiliated, all fight went out of the young man and he stayed where he had landed, his head sagging, as if the weight of his humiliation was too much for him to bear. The Kid stepped over to him, and bending down, took the six-gun still resting in Hunnicut's holster. He was about to tear the tin star from Hunnicut's shirt when Longarm saw Denton stop him.

"Hell, Kid, leave him have the badge," said Denton, loud enough for all to hear. "He's still the town marshal. He ain't done nothing wrong. Not now he ain't."

Then Denton stepped out of the doorway and waved the Kid into the jail, and as Hunnicut got to his feet and slunk off, the Kid brought out a balding, terrified man in his early fifties, his wrists handcuffed behind him. The Kid was prodding his spine with Hunnicut's six-gun.

As the man started down the jail's steps, blinking up into the brilliant setting sun, a woman's scream pierced the hushed stillness of the crowded plaza. It was Clairborn's wife. Longarm glanced over at the knot of womenfolk in the doorway and saw the women struggling to keep her from darting away from them and rushing to her husband's side.

The dazed, terrified storekeeper seemed not to have heard his wife's scream. Aware that nothing on God's green earth was going to rise up and smite his enemies —that he was going to die as surely as the sun was setting—he began to tremble violently, his lips quivering with abject, naked terror. As he neared the oak tree, his knees buckled, and the Kid had to struggle to keep him on his feet.

Denton motioned brusquely to one of the other two gunslicks. The man hurried over and grabbed the storekeeper's arm, holding him upright until he and the Kid could boost him up onto the barrel, where Slade slipped the noose over the man's head and jumped down.

"My God!" cried Jane. "They're really going to do it!"

She turned and bolted back into the office. As Longarm followed after her, he took one swift glimpse back and saw the barrel rolling across the ground, the storekeeper twisting slowly in midair, his head at an odd, grotesque angle, his face already turning dark.

The last sound Longarm heard as he closed the door behind him was a high, piercing cry of anguish.

Clairborn's wife.

Chapter 4

Without a single glance back at the dead man dancing on air behind him, Denton strode purposefully along the plaza and kept going until he reached the Silverado. He felt all eyes on him, but refused to acknowledge those crowding around. He was in no mood to banter with these spineless bastards, and the last thing he wanted was their sweaty palms clapping him on the back, telling him what a great man he was. Not a one of them had the courage to face the day without a bellyful of rotgut, and all he felt for them was a fathomless contempt.

His reaction to the hanging had been more severe than he had expected; he could still hear that fool woman's scream. Even more unsettling had been his confrontation with that kid marshal. Denton hadn't expected him to stand up to him like that, and he was uneasy that he had been forced to humiliate the kid in front of the town. But it was Hunnicut's own damn fault; the kid shouldn't have dealt himself into a game if he couldn't ante up.

He pushed on through the saloon and up the rear stairs to his expansive town headquarters. He pushed through a door off the balcony into an inner hallway, passed his large sitting room, then his bedroom, and continued on down the hallway to his office, a powerful stench of cigar smoke alerting him to Hook's presence. The man in black was sitting in Denton's soft, leather armchair in the corner, his feet up on a hard-backed chair, a gleaming new Winchester leaning against the paneled wall beside him.

Denton moved behind his desk and slumped down into his armchair. He looked speculatively at Hook. "I see you got a new rifle."

"I lost the other one."

"Too bad. You put great store by it."

"A rifle's a tool, and a tool is no better than the man using it."

"The doc says Ben Tomlinson is in no danger of losing his life from that slug you put in him, and that new stage of theirs is still in use. It pulled out late this afternoon. Don't look like the delay had much of an effect on their schedule." The words were spoken casually, almost idly, but Hook had no difficulty catching the implied criticism.

"I ran into some trouble."

"I'm listening."

Hook tossed his cigar into a brass spittoon. The sound of it sizzling out filled the small office. "A tall drink of water was up on the box beside Tomlinson, fellow dressed in brown. A greenhorn, I thought, but he kept after me and I had to leave Tomlinson with only one bullet in him."

"Where is he now?"

"He's the one drove the stage in. He came in downstairs, had himself some whiskey, kept his mouth shut, and took a room at the hotel. Last I saw, he was entering the stage line office."

Denton leaned forward intently. "You think maybe Tomlinson sent for him? You think he's a hired gun?"

Hook smiled. "Not Tomlinson. And his daughter wouldn't hear of such a thing. More'n likely he was up on the box with Tomlinson, so he dealt himself in when the shooting began. He wasn't too smart. Came after me with a six-gun and I had a rifle."

"Only now he has your rifle."

Hook didn't like that. He moved slightly in his chair and let his hooded eyes rest coldly on Denton. "I'll get the rifle back."

"All right. You didn't kill Tomlinson, and you didn't put that stage out of commission, but you sure as hell gave Tomlinson and his daughter something to think about. So maybe that's enough for now."

Hook stood up. "I'll be at my place."

"If I need you, I'll send the swamper over."

Hook nodded and left. Leaning back in his chair, Denton listened intently, but he could not hear the son of a bitch's footsteps on the hard, polished floor as he walked down the hall. Denton didn't even hear the door close behind him. He waited a moment or two, then got up and peered down the hall. It was empty.

He felt cold all of a sudden and reached into a drawer for his whiskey flask.

As the kitchen window darkened, Longarm sat at the kitchen table discussing with Jane the situation in Sand Hills. She was a somber young lady, and the discussion had not been an easy one. Jane was doing little to hide her disappointment with the town—and with Longarm, too, he sensed—for not having done something to stop what had happened. Longarm himself was unhappy that his undercover role had forced him to keep a low profile, at least for now.

Tomlinson called hoarsely from his bedroom. Jane hurried in to see to him and came back smiling. Her father was hungry. As Jane busied herself at the stove, Longarm went into the bedroom, sat down on the edge of the wounded man's bed, and told him about the lynching. When he finished, Tomlinson stirred unhappily and looked gloomily out the window. It was the kind of news that could indeed cast a pall over a man. Tomlinson had known the storekeeper personally and had liked him. It was probably beginning to look to Tomlinson as if he and his daughter were trying to run a stagecoach line in the bowels of Dante's Inferno.

Jane appeared in the doorway.

"Drake, it looks like we've got visitors."

"Who?" asked Tomlinson.

"Denton."

"That son of a bitch!" the man said, stirring angrily.

"Stay right where you are, Dad," Jane said firmly. "Drake and I can handle him."

"No one runs my errands!"

"Lay back," snapped Longarm. "You're in no condition to take on that vulture. Trust your daughter to handle this. She's done all right so far."

"You heard him, Dad."

"I'm still hungry," Tomlinson groused.

Jane smiled in relief. "There's fresh coffee on the stove, and some beans I was heating up."

Jane glanced sharply at Longarm and left the room. Longarm followed out after her as she hurried down the stairs to the warehouse. Fred, still wearing his green eyeshade, was standing uneasily with Denton and the two men with him—the Kid and Slade Cullen.

"Thank you, Fred," Jane said, dismissing him.

As the nervous clerk hurried off, Denton touched the brim of his hat in deference to Jane. "Sorry to hear about your trouble, Jane."

"What trouble?" she snapped angrily.

"Why, I heard someone shot your horses from their traces and punched some holes in your stage."

"And shot my father."

"That's what I meant. I was very sorry to hear that. How is your father?"

"He's fine, no thanks to you," she snapped.

"That's not very kind, Jane."

Jane was doing a slow burn. "What are you doing here, Denton?" she demanded icily. "You must be all worn out. You had a very busy afternoon."

Unfazed, Denton smiled blandly. "I'm here because I'm concerned, Jane. Judging from what happened to your father this morning, and the damage to your new stage, it sounds like this line needs protection."

49

Jane's face crimsoned. "Yes, it *does* need protection from a vile bastard like you. Mark my words, Denton. You'll live to regret what you did out there on that plaza today—and what your hired gun did to my father. I am amazed you have the gall to come here and face me. Have you no shame!"

The Kid and Slade Cullen looked at Denton uneasily. But Denton kept his affable manner, though Longarm saw it was becoming a mite difficult. The man apparently had a thick hide when having one served his purpose.

"I don't know what you're runnin' on about, Jane," he told her, his voice reasonable and calm. "All I came here to do was offer you protection from trouble. That's something I should think you'd be very eager to have."

Before Jane could reply, Longarm stepped up beside her. "Just how much would this protection cost, Mr. Denton?" he asked politely.

Frowning, Denton turned to face Longarm. "Who're you, mister?"

"Name's Drake, and I been thinkin' of buying into the Sand Hills Mountain Line."

"You sure that's what you want, after what happened today?"

"But, if as you say, you can see to it that such things will not happen again, why not? This is a very successful line, and will remain so. As Jane has explained it to me, there's little likelihood of future competition." Longarm smiled blandly, as Denton had a moment before.

Denton looked at Longarm shrewdly. "And all you want to know is how much my protection will cost?"

"Precisely."

Frowning, Denton rubbed his hand across his chin in sudden reflection. "Well, now," he said after a moment, "I think thirty percent of what the line pulls in should do it—for a starter."

Longarm kept his eyes from showing anything—anything at all—as he pretended to consider the amount. Then he looked at Denton. "Thirty percent is a great deal, Mr. Denton."

Denton seemed suddenly amused at Longarm. "Why not look at it this way, Drake. You've got to weigh that amount against the chance of running into so much trouble you'll wind up bankrupt."

"But thirty percent. That will barely leave us enough to operate on."

"Well, now, it ain't as bad as all that. We keep tabs on your books. If we find our modest percentage is cutting into your operating costs, you'll find us ready to lower our charges." Denton smiled. "After all, we don't want to put you out of business."

"That's very kind of you. But don't you think you should leave us with some profits, too?"

"You've got to think of the future," replied Denton, by now the epitome of restraint and sound reason. "At this time the county's pretty lawless. But that'll change in time. When it's finally law-abiding and peaceful around here, there won't be any need for my protection. Then I'll move on to other enterprises, and you'll be left with a going business. *Then* you can start making profits."

The man was so brazen, it was almost an art. Longarm was amused. But only for a minute. He glanced at Jane. She was handling herself beautifully. At first it must have sounded as if he had gone mad, especially

51

when she heard his overly polite tone as he discussed this outright, brazen extortion with Denton; but she had not batted an eye, and now she was letting him have full rein.

"What you say is perfectly true," Longarm admitted to Denton. "But I have no idea how long that would take."

"Yep. Can't argue with you on that. Might take years, the way things are around here—with that silver mine, and all."

"Years, you say?"

"Yeah, years. But you know what they say, Drake. Better late than never."

"You have a point there." Longarm appeared to be considering the offer. He glanced at Denton. "Give Jane and me—and Mr. Tomlinson—some time to think this over, will you? I know Jane sounded very angry just now, but surely you can understand her concern for her father's safety."

"I tell you what, Drake. I'll come by another time. Maybe something'll happen to make you want to hurry things along."

"You're not making a threat, are you?"

Denton held up both hands in mock horror. "Of course not, Drake! Like you, I'm just thinkin' of Jane, and this stage line. It's a damn fine investment if it doesn't get all shot up and you find you can't meet your schedules. I'm sure you understand."

That was all Jane could take. Stepping angrily in front of Longarm, she snapped, "Don't worry, Denton. He understands. And so do I. You're giving us a few days before you send that hired killer after one of our stages again. You've made that perfectly clear. Now get out, and take your hired dogs with you!"

With a curt nod to Longarm, Denton turned on his heels and left, his two gunslicks following after him. As soon as they were gone, Longarm hurried upstairs. Parting the curtains slightly in Tomlinson's bedroom, he peered across the alley, studying the dim area beyond the back fence of the wagon yard. After a few seconds, he spotted what he was looking for—a tall, gaunt man in a black suit, standing in the shadows. He was holding a carbine. As Longarm watched, the man shifted in the shadowy niche, and vanished.

Longarm turned to face Jane. She had raced up the stairs just behind him and stood now at his elbow. "He was out there," he told her. "Hook. He was watching this place, in case Denton got into any trouble."

"That so?"

"Yes, Jane. He was out there."

"I don't care what you just saw. I want you to explain yourself."

"You mean about what I told Denton?"

"Mr. Drake, you said nothing, absolutely nothing, to me or Dad about becoming a partner in this line. And if you're seriously thinking of giving those vultures any part of our business, forget it."

Longarm grinned at her. "Why not call me Jud."

"Hey, wait a minute," cried Tomlinson. "Ain't no one goin' to tell me what happened with Denton?"

Ignoring Tomlinson's plea, Longarm looked at Jane. "Now, Jane, do you mean you really don't know what I was up to?"

She softened then, a mischievous gleam in her eyes.

53

"You were only pretending to consider Denton's offer . . . to gain time?"

"Precisely."

"But time for what?"

"To look the situation over, see what options you might have. And to wait for them to make another move, and maybe this time a mistake."

"Does that mean you're *not* buying into the line?"

"No one's asked me yet. But for the moment at least, that's a mite premature."

He strode past her on his way out of the bedroom.

"Where are you going?"

"I'm going to take a look around Sand Hills. The place interests me. Especially if there's a chance it'll be my new home."

Tomlinson had sat up in his bed. "Is anyone going to tell me what happened down there?" he wailed.

"Tell him," Longarm told Jane, and left.

For the next hour or so, Longarm wandered in and out of saloons, stores, and other buildings until he had engraved in his mind the layout of every building, street, and alley immediately adjoining the stage line office. As he walked down the streets and back alleys, he did not fail to notice the few Denton gunslicks he passed. They were easy enough to recognize, since they were the only men carrying side arms, in blatant disregard of the ordinance the town marshal had sought so unsuccessfully to cite earlier.

Longarm moved down a few blocks and found himself in the district where most of the activity concerning the silver mine was centered. What with all the freighters, cowhands, nesters, and commercial travelers stopping over on their way through the pass, even at this hour there was plenty of activity to observe. The saloons, parlor houses, and gambling halls were all crowded and noisy, many of them so recently thrown up that the outside walls were not yet painted. The streets and narrow alleys were filled with swaggering, liquored-up miners and freighters moving from one house or gambling hall to another.

And here too were more of Denton's men, in greater numbers, most of them lugging shotguns and keeping order in a rough, brutal way—but keeping order. Everywhere Longarm looked they were strategically placed to enable them to handle any full-scale uproar that might arise.

He ended up finally in the Silverado. The place was crowded and it was obvious that this, too, was a part of Denton's growing commercial empire. He probably had a sizable investment as well in many of the newly built parlor houses. Indeed, as Longarm paused inside the batwings to look the place over more carefully than he had when he came in that afternoon, he spotted the gambler he had brought in with the stage. Undoubtedly, the girls he had had with him were upstairs now in their cribs hard at work, or in one of the parlor houses in the red-light district farther down.

The saloon took up the entire ground floor of the building and appeared to be the best-guarded place in town. A man with a carbine sat in a chair at the top of the stairs, his ankles resting on the rail as he watched the activity below. On the saloon floor itself two gunmen wandered around keeping an eye on every faro and monte dealer, and all the poker tables. A sawed-off shotgun was on prominent display on a rack behind the bar, and Longarm had no doubt that a shorter, more devastating variety was resting just under the bar in case of an emergency.

Striding over to the bar, ignoring the curious glances of those he brushed aside, Longarm ordered a whiskey, paid for the bottle, and took it to a table against the far wall. It was while he was threading himself through the crowd that he spotted James B. Hook, the man he had hoped to find.

Dressed in a somber, funereal black, Hook was smoking a cigar as he sat at a small table in a far corner of the place, his new rifle leaning against the wall beside him. A bottle and shot glass sat on the table before him, but Hook did not appear to be drinking as his lidded, reptilian gaze flicked over the saloon. He looked like an ancient lizard crouched on a rock, waiting for an insect to come within reach of his darting tongue. Despite the crowd in the place, Longarm noticed the two tables on either side of Hook were empty, as if he had created about him a zone that repelled all normal human activities, or feelings.

Longarm slumped back in his chair and did his best to kill the bottle. It had been a wild day and he was trying to settle down some so he could rein in his racing thoughts—and try not to see too often in his mind's eye the slowly twisting body of that storekeeper. Longarm had planned to arrive quietly in this place, get his bearings, and then make his move. Instead, he had found himself—as usual—thrust deeply into a local squabble. If he had intended to maintain a low profile, he had failed miserably.

As the noise of the place increased, intruding into his thoughts like an insistent hammer, he decided it was time for him to get some shut-eye. He brought his bottle back to the bar and left the saloon. As he pushed through the batwings, he glanced back into the corner.

James B. Hook had vanished.

But that didn't mean he wasn't still around.

Chapter 5

Longarm slept late the next morning, and not wanting to impose on Jane, ate his breakfast at a small restaurant across the street from the hotel. Then he walked over to the stage line where he strolled idly about looking over the coaches, after which he entered the stables and inspected the coach horses stamping thunderously in their stalls. He spoke for a while with the two stable boys, Len and Syd, and with Andy, the old cowpoke in charge. Two of the drivers bunked in the rear of the horse barn, and he stopped in to chat with them for a while. In short, he was playing the part of a man seriously considering buying into the enterprise. A little before the noon hour he borrowed a saddle horse from Andy and rode out of town.

He always liked to get some idea of the surrounding country whenever he was on an assignment, and what he found now as he put Sand Hills behind him was a dry land, unpleasantly so, swept by a wind that blew continuously, sending tiny daggers of dust into his eyes. After about ten miles, he reached the foothills of the mountains and began lifting into cooler air. Before long he found himself riding over a surprisingly lush, sweeping grassland flanked by pine-clothed bluffs and steep-sided hills.

After a few more miles, he pulled up on a small ridge and found that the lush grasslands extended as far as the eye could see. He now understood perfectly Frank Ellison's desire to keep this land from being torn up by nesters' plows. He could understand as well why many less-favored ranchers would consider it fair game to appropriate Circle D cattle for their own less well endowed herds.

He got back to Sand Hills late that afternoon and decided to find out how Tomlinson was doing. Entering the bedroom with Jane, Longarm found Tomlinson in the act of getting out of bed to test himself. He was dressed in a long cotton nightgown and his gray hair was comically awry. But Longarm did not smile as he watched the older man grasp a bedpost and haul himself carefully upright.

Longarm moved over by the window to get out of Tomlinson's way as he began to pad shakily about the room. Jane watched nervously. It was clear her father was still weak from loss of blood, and that a man his age did not so easily shrug off the effects of a gunshot wound, no matter how superficial. Puffing wearily, Tomlinson slumped back down onto his bed.

"Guess I need to rest up some more," he admitted ruefully, glancing at Jane, then at Longarm.

"I'm just glad you're up and able to move around," Jane told him, sitting beside him and draping an arm over his shoulder. Then she kissed him affectionately on the cheek.

"You don't have to rush it, Tommy," Longarm said. "Jane's doing fine. She's taken that damaged stage off the line and has brought it into the yard downstairs. Tomorrow we'll start repairing those holes. It'll be as good as new before long."

"Not as good as new," Jane corrected him unhappily. "We'll never get that ripped upholstery to look right. Eventually, we'll have to rip out those seats and put in new ones."

Tomlinson looked at Longarm shrewdly. "Drake, I heard tell you was lookin' this outfit over this morning."

"I was. After all, if I'm a potential buyer, I should nose around some. Right?"

"You think you can stall Denton for long?"

"Not long, but maybe long enough."

"You got any kind of plan?"

"I'm working on it."

"No need to badger him, Dad," Jane said. "There's no reason why he should stick his nose out for us."

"He already has."

Longarm glanced at Jane. "Did I smell coffee when I came up here?"

Jane brightened and got to her feet. "You did, indeed."

Longarm glanced back at Tomlinson. "Rest up, Tommy. I'll be in to see you again tomorrow."

"Sure, Drake. Didn't mean to push you."

"Forget it."

Longarm could tell Jane was anxious to give him

some news she did not wish to share with her father for fear of upsetting him. He sat down before a platter stacked high with doughnuts and watched her bring over a coffeepot from the stove.

"All right, Jane. What's up?"

"Are you willing to help us, to see that nothing like that lynching ever happens again in this town?"

"I'm willing to help you. Let's leave it at that. Now what's this all about?"

She finished pouring their coffee and sat down opposite him. "There's going to be a meeting in Ben Blue's dry-goods store down the street tonight. A secret meeting, some of the town's businessmen and homesteaders from nearby. That lynching yesterday shook them up pretty bad. We're going to try to figure some way we can get together against Denton."

Longarm cocked an eyebrow. *"We?"*

"You said you're willing to help."

"I didn't say I'd go to any meeting. And I don't think you should go, either."

Her mouth tightened. "Oh? And why not?"

"Because it will only be a waste of time."

"How can you be so sure?"

Longarm's smile was cynical. "Think back to yesterday. The plaza in front of that jail was crowded with upset townsmen and homesteaders. But they didn't come to stop a lynching. They were there to watch. Not one of them raised a hand. Before a man as ruthless as Denton, they're helpless, and all the meetings in the world won't change that."

"You don't seem to have much faith in your fellow citizens."

"Not those fellow citizens. They lack what I'd call a

damned essential quality for standing up to a man like Denton. Backbone. If you let yourself get mixed up with those rabbits, it might give you and your father additional problems, and you've already got enough."

"But don't you think we should do something?"

"Waiting, biding your time, and getting yourselves ready *is* doing something."

"Biding our time? For what?"

He looked at her for a long moment. He never liked to telegraph a punch, and it always sounded silly to reveal a plan of action beforehand. He would wait until he was ready. There'd be time enough then to let her in on what he had in mind.

He reached for a doughnut. "These are delicious, Jane. How about another cup of coffee."

She knew he was stalling, but she could see it would do her no good to press him. Without commenting, she lifted the coffeepot and filled his cup.

"Have you heard anything about the town marshal?" Longarm asked.

"I heard this morning he was holed up in his room, too ashamed to show his face." She shook her head. "I don't blame him."

"Where's his room?"

"At the hotel, a small room in back over the kitchen. He gets a special rate, him being the town marshal. Why? You thinking of paying him a visit?"

"I think maybe there'll come a time when we'll need him."

"Jimmy Hunnicut? Why, Jud, you know he's finished around here."

"Don't be so sure of that. Maybe we can do something to restore his reputation."

"Is this what you're biding your time for, a crazy idea like that?"

"I'm not sure yet."

She sighed and finished her coffee.

"You going to that meeting?" Longarm asked.

"No," she said wearily, "I guess not."

"Good."

Longarm left Jane's apartment a few minutes later to visit a barbershop for a shave, trim, and a bath, after which he returned to his hotel room, changed, and ate his supper in the hotel dining room.

After the meal he approached the desk clerk and asked where Hunnicut's room was, and was directed to a narrow back hallway on the second floor. He found Hunnicut's room at the end of it and knocked on the door. There was no answer to his knock, but he heard the squeak of a bedspring and something that sounded like an empty bottle strike the floor.

He knocked again, harder, the force of his blows causing the door to swing open a few inches. He pushed it out of his way and walked in. A kerosene lamp was sitting on a dresser, its light filtering faintly through the soot-blackened chimney, casting a feeble glow over the man sprawled facedown on his bare mattress. Hunnicut was out cold with his boots, pants, and shirt still on. The smell emanating from the prone figure was sour and fetid, compounded of cheap whiskey and stale vomit.

Longarm walked over to the cot and shook Hunnicut's shoulder. He got no response. The marshal was breathing, his breath rank enough to stop a grandfather clock at twenty paces. But he was so deep in an alcoholic stupor, so completely out of it, that it was doubtful Longarm could get him awake, short of detonating a cannon under his bed. Which meant Hunnicut wouldn't be going anywhere soon.

Longarm turned and left the man, closing the door firmly and waiting for the latch bolt to click into the door frame before moving off.

On his way to the stables a moment later, he was passing the darkened express office when he glimpsed Jane standing inside it near a corner window. He mounted the low porch, knocked once on the door and entered. Jane pulled him over to the window and pointed toward a storefront farther down.

"That's the dry-goods store," she told him.

"Blue's holding the meeting now?"

"Yes."

Longarm said nothing, content to watch, wondering grimly just how secret this meeting actually was. Out of the darkness of the plaza two portly storekeepers hurried, heading for Blue's store. Better late than never.

"I still don't feel good about not being there," Jane said, as the two men disappeared into the store. "Ben didn't say anything when I told him I wasn't going to show up, but I could tell from the look on his face he thought I was scared of Denton."

"Being scared of Denton makes damned good sense. Denton has all the men and all the guns."

Tensing suddenly, Jane said, "Look . . . !"

Longarm leaned closer to the window and saw a group of armed men emerging from the shadows farther down the street. They were coming straight for Ben Blue's dry-goods store.

Jane turned from the window and started to move past Longarm. His hand shot out and caught her wrist, stopping her.

"Where do you think you're going?"

She tried to pull free of his grasp. "Let me go! Maybe I can warn Ben and the others! I'll slip in through the back!"

"It's too late," Longarm told her. "The way Denton operates, there's bound to be more of his men already behind the store. And I don't see Hook. Which means he's watching this whole operation from a dark shadow somewhere with his new rifle."

Jane's shoulders slumped and she stopped struggling. Longarm looked out again, Jane moving up beside him. Denton's men had reached the front of Blue's store. Longarm counted five men in all as they ranged themselves in a semicircle in front of the store, waiting.

The door of the dry-goods store burst open and men began stumbling out—the unarmed men who'd been attending this supposedly secret meeting. Longarm tried to count them as they came out and gave up. He was sure there were more than a dozen. When they saw Denton's gunmen blocking their way, they came to a wary halt.

Then the Kid came out, a revolver in his hand, and stared insolently at the trembling cluster of frightened townsmen. He didn't say anything to them and he didn't threaten them with his revolver. It was not necessary. Under that young killer's gaze, not a single man dared to move.

"Where's Ben Blue?" Longarm asked. "He come out yet?"

"No," Jane replied, her voice dead. "Ben's still in there."

Abruptly Slade Cullen emerged from the store. The Kid joined him and waved the townsmen away, barking a warning to them as he did so. Hastily the townsmen slipped away through the ring of gunmen, scattering toward their homes. Slade and the Kid watched them go for a second or two, then started off up the street, the rest of the gunmen following behind them.

As soon as they were gone, Longarm left the stage office, sprinted down the street, and ducked into the dry-goods store, Jane hard on his heels. A man lay sprawled on his back on the floor just inside the door, his face smashed and bleeding, his clothes torn. His right arm was bent at so grotesque an angle that Longarm doubted the fracture could ever be made right.

Longarm heard Jane's strangled gasp as he knelt beside the unconscious storekeeper.

"Get the doctor," he told her through clenched teeth.

She turned and ran back out of the store.

Blue was breathing through his bloodied, open mouth. His nose had been crushed. His front teeth were broken stumps. Through his ripped shirt, livid, swelling bruises were already beginning to rise on his frail chest. He looked like he had fallen down a flight of stairs—a long flight.

Carefully and gently, Longarm lifted him and carried him into the back of the store, looking for the storekeeper's living quarters. He found a large room and entered, stretching the man's limp figure onto what was apparently his cot, marveling as he did at how little the

67

store owner weighed. The thought of what it must have been like for this frail, birdlike man to stand up to Slade Cullen's bludgeoning blows sent a chill up Longarm's spine. And in that instant he knew he would not leave this town without first seeing to it that Slade Cullen suffered in the same way that he had made the store-keeper suffer.

Longarm had just finished lighting two more kerosene lamps to provide additional light for the doctor when Jane hurried into the store with him. As Jane and the doctor took over, Longarm pulled out a cheroot and walked outside to light up. About five minutes later Jane joined him. She was seething.

"What kind of a man could do that to another human?" she asked, her voice trembling.

"A man who's lacking something, Jane. Something at the core. He might look human, but he's not really human, not at all."

"And all those men! They did nothing."

"They were unarmed."

"But they could have done something, said something. They just stood there."

"Stop it, Jane. You'll drive yourself crazy going on like this. Put it behind you. Blue must have known what the dangers were when he called this meeting."

"No," she said, shaking her head sadly. "I don't think he could have, not really."

Longarm tossed the stump of his cheroot into the street. "Good night, Jane."

"Good night, Jud."

As Longarm moved off, he saw Jane turn and go back inside to continue helping the doctor. He had hoped she would not do that. She was upset enough

68

already. But he knew there was nothing he could do to stop her. As for himself, he was going to have a few drinks and do some thinking. It had occurred to him that he had come to Sand Hills to get one man, James B. Hook—not to salvage a stage line or set a town to rights.

Somehow he was going to have to figure out a way to fit James B. Hook into his plans while he set about saving these fool storekeepers from the likes of Bull Denton.

The next morning Longarm prevailed upon Jane to leave her duties in the stage office and come with him to Jimmy Hunnicut's room. She was not anxious to go with him. But she understood Longarm had something in mind, and keeping to herself any misgivings she might have had, she accompanied him to the town marshal's room and stood aside as Longarm knocked on his door.

Again there was no response. Longarm knocked twice more on the door, but got no reply. He turned the doorknob and pushed open the door. Nothing much had changed, except for the fact that the kerosene lamp was out now, the only light coming in through the room's single window.

"My God," Jane said, coming unhappily in after Longarm. "The smell."

"Why not open that window?"

She did so promptly, then joined Longarm standing beside the cot. The young town marshal's face was turned to the wall, one arm hanging loosely over the edge of the cot, his mouth slack as he breathed heavily through it. Jane looked appalled as she noted the empty bottles scattered about everywhere, and as she moved closer to peer down at Hunnicut, her foot kicked a bottle, sending it spinning against another one under the cot.

Jane spoke in a hushed whisper. "Emmy Glover, the cleaning lady, told me this morning he hasn't been out of the room once since the lynching. He's been sending down for his meals. He's only had two that she knows of, and he's left the tray outside the door with most of the food untouched."

"It's about what I figured. When you're this deep into booze, food is the last thing you want."

Jane shivered. And Longarm did not blame her. Hunnicut's sodden figure was not a pleasant sight. His red hair was wild, his face mottled with red stubble, and his eyes were lost in dark shadows. He slept on, oblivious of their presence.

Longarm walked over to the door and deliberately slammed it shut. The room rocked from the sound, but it had no apparent effect on Hunnicut. He slept on, breathing heavily, not stirring a muscle. Longarm returned to the cot then and began prodding Hunnicut with his fingers. He was not gentle, but still the sprawled figure did not respond. Leaning over him, Longarm slapped his face, hard. Hunnicut stirred a little, moving his legs some and drawing his hand up off the floor. But his eyes did not open.

Longarm looked at Jane. "This is why I wanted you to come with me. He was like this last night. You'll have to work on him. It's going to be a job. Get a bucket of water and a towel. Dump the water on him and work on his face with the towel till he comes around enough for you to pour coffee into him. Make the coffee hot and strong, and—"

"Jud! I now how to handle a drunk. I was married to one!"

Longarm smiled faintly. "Good for you, then. You must tell me about that husband of yours sometime. He was a goddamn fool to let a woman like you get away."

She blushed at his unexpected compliment.

"Anyway, I'd sure appreciate it if you could get him sobered up enough to eat something solid. When he's fit enough to sit up and listen to what I have in mind for him, let me know."

"You're not going to help me?"

Longarm shook his head. "It's going to take awhile for you to pull him out of this. One of us should stay close to the office, and it better be me. Denton's bound to get impatient. He might decide to give us another nudge, to remind us of the advantages of his protection."

"And what will you tell him if he does visit?"

Longarm shrugged. "I'll know that when the time comes."

He went out, leaving her with the sodden deputy, not envying her the task he had dropped in her lap. He left the hotel and, reaching the office, saw that Fred was hard at work at his desk, his inevitable green eyeshade an effective barrier between him and the rest of the world. Longarm could hear the carpenters in back working on the stage. Nodding to the clerk, he passed on into the warehouse and stood on the loading platform while he watched the coachmen working, remembering Jane's lament that little could be done about the upholstery torn up by Hook's bullets. Then he went on upstairs to the apartment.

Tomlinson was dressed and in the kitchen, shoveling down fried eggs and potatoes, a big mug of hot coffee beside his dish. He looked up as Longarm entered, and Longarm noted that a lot of the man's color had come back, though his cheeks were still sunken somewhat, his eyes a little dull.

"I'm up and dressed," Tomlinson announced, proud of himself. "Where's Jane?"

Longarm took a cup from a cupboard, poured himself some coffee, and sat down at the table across from Tomlinson. "She's at the hotel, doing what she can to sober up the town marshal."

"Hunnicut?" he snorted. "Why the hell's she bothering?"

"I think we're going to need him."

"You must be off your feed."

"I admit he's no good to us now. But I figure all he needs is someone to stand by him for a while, prop him up some. He showed guts the other day, standing up to Denton as long as he did."

Tomlinson pushed away his empty plate. "From what I heard, he covered himself with shit. As a lawman, he isn't worth a pinch of coon shit."

"Jesus, Tomlinson, what would you have done in such a spot?"

"Why, I would've—"

"Stow it," Longarm said, holding up his hand impatiently. "You don't know what the hell you would have done. And besides, the kid's hardly twenty. He needs seasoning."

"Well, he won't get the chance for that around here, I'm thinking. He's finished in this town."

"That's what he thinks, too. But maybe we can convince him that ain't true."

"What do you mean, it's not true?"

"Finish your coffee. We'll talk about this later. Right now, why don't you go downstairs and take a walk around the premises? Show yourself. Let people know you're in charge again."

"Why?"

"Just do it."

Tomlinson looked at Longarm for a long moment, his gaze shrewd. "You know, mister, you came in here talking about buying a hotel. You let on you were a gambler. But it seems to me you're a whole hell of a lot more than a gambler. What's your angle? Who are you, anyway?"

"Right now, Tommy, I'm a gambler. Anyone who'd hang in here and try to get this line's chestnuts out of the fire would have to be a gambler, wouldn't you say?"

"You want me to think you're a drifter. But you ain't. Dammit, I know you ain't."

Longarm grinned and took out a cheroot and lit up. "I told you, Tommy, I'm a gambler. Just let it go at that."

"You really plannin' on buying into this stage line?"

"Don't know the first thing about a stagecoach line. I told you before, a hotel's more my speed, along with pretty girls, a well-stocked bar, and plenty of games of chance." Longarm took out his bent and worn deck of cards and began shuffling them with a dexterity that immediately impressed Tomlinson.

Tomlinson shrugged. "Have it your way," he said, getting to his feet.

Without any further conversation with Longarm he washed his plate off in the bucket standing in the sink, wiped his hands on the dish towel, and left the apartment. Longarm paused in his game of solitaire to listen carefully as the older man cautiously descended the stairs.

Tomlinson was pushing it, maybe, getting up so soon. But he was a tough man to keep down, which meant Longarm could maybe count on him when the showdown came—and come it would. Denton was not a man you could stall for very long.

Longarm was growing weary of his game of solitaire and had just about finished his second cheroot when he heard Jane's light feet on the stairs. A moment later she pushed into the apartment and entered the kitchen. Her braided crown of chestnut hair was coming loose, and unruly strands were poking out; her face was pale and drawn. Sobering up the young town marshal had been a difficult, unpleasant task, as Longarm had known it would be.

"Jim Hunnicut's back among the living," she told Longarm wearily.

"Nice going," Longarm told her, scooping up his cards. "You look like *you* could use a drink."

"No, thank you," she said firmly, slumping down at the table.

"Has he eaten anything?"

"Yes. But he still looks pretty green around the gills."

74

"What's he up to now?"

"He's packing his bags. From what he told me, he'll be leaving on our next stage out."

Pocketing the deck of cards, Longarm stood up and put his hat on. "Guess I'll go over and have a talk with him."

"Jud, what's the use? Let the poor kid get out of here. He can start a new life somewhere else."

"Sure, Jane. That's what everyone thinks when they begin to run. But there's no place far enough when you're running from yourself."

Longarm left the apartment.

Pushing into Hunnicut's room without knocking, Longarm saw the young man busy stuffing shirts into his saddlebags. He spun around at Longarm's entrance, his face tight with fear. When he saw it was Longarm, he relaxed somewhat, the fear turning to an edgy anger.

"Who the hell are you, mister?"

"Name's Jud. Jud Drake. I'm thinking of buying into the Sand Hills Mountain Line with Tomlinson and his daughter."

"You're the one sent Jane over here."

"Thought maybe we should talk, but we couldn't do that in the condition you were in."

"I don't see what you and me got to talk about."

"Why not sit down and give me a chance to see if maybe we do."

Hunnicut looked awful, the way a man usually does after a three-day bender. He was probably seeing Longarm through a pounding headache, which was doing nothing to sweeten his disposition. He sat wearily back on the edge of his cot, a folded cotton shirt in his hand.

"I'm listening, mister. But make it short. I got a stage to catch."

"You're sure that's the thing to do, are you?"

"I'm finished here. I found out I wasn't the man for the job. When push came to shove, I gave out. A man's dead because I didn't have the sand to stop Denton."

"A man's dead because Denton had you outgunned. And because not a single townsman stepped forward to side you. Denton knew you were not going to shoot him because he knew you were not a damned fool. And you would have been if you traded fire with Denton. Even if you had killed Denton, the rest of his crew would have been alive and Dean Clairborn would hang in spite of anything you did."

Hunnicut shook his head stubbornly. "I was wearing a badge. I had no choice but to shoot, and I didn't."

"I won't argue the matter with you," Longarm told him. "I'm offering you a chance to start all over again, here in Sand Hills. I'm offering you a chance to help me stop Denton."

"What in the hell are you talking about? You saw what he did to me. You know how many guns he has backing him. And just now before you barged in, the cleaning woman told me what his men did to Ben Blue last night."

"Well, doesn't that make you want to stop the son of a bitch?"

"What am I supposed to do? Cut him down with a

76

sawed-off shotgun when he crosses in front of an alley?"

"You're still legally the law in this town. I want you to join forces with me and Tomlinson."

"You and old man Tomlinson?" Hunnicut was astounded at the apparent absurdity of Longarm's proposal. "Mister, you must be crazy."

Longarm pulled up a hard-backed chair and straddled it, folding his arms on the back of it. "Listen to me, Hunnicut. The three of us can make a difference. I mean it. I've been in situations a whole hell of a lot worse than this."

Hunnicut's eyes narrowed. "You have?"

"Yes, I have. And so, I'll bet, has Tomlinson."

"Who are you, Drake? Where are you from, anyway?"

"That's not important. Just trust me."

"Why should I?"

"Because you really have no option. If you leave here now, you'll be running out with your tail between your legs, a whipped cur. Stay, and you'll be fighting back. What the hell have you got to lose?"

Hunnicut frowned. And Longarm could see he had made his point. Hunnicut had already lost something without which no man could long survive—his self-respect. He'd been beaten down in public, and because of his shameful capitulation an innocent man had ended his days twisting on the end of a rope.

"What do you want me to do?" Hunnicut asked, squaring his shoulders, a tiny glint of defiance showing now in his eyes.

Longarm stood up, swinging the chair away, and started for the door. "Stay, that's all. For now. Like I said, you're still the law in this town. We're going to use that fact when the time comes."

"When will that be?"

"Soon. I promise you."

Longarm opened the door and left Hunnicut still sitting on the cot and looking a lot better than he had when Longarm entered. Something had transformed him.

Hope.

The clerk was outside in the street, helping load a stagecoach, when Longarm strode into the office and beckoned to Jane.

"Where's you father?" he asked.

"He went upstairs a little while ago. Said he was all wore out. But he looks so much better, Jud."

"Yes, he does."

"Did you have that talk you wanted with Jimmy?"

"I did. Looks like he won't be taking that stage tonight after all."

"What on earth did you say to him?"

"That his best course of action would be to stay here and throw in with us."

"Us?"

"You, your father, and me."

"That's a pretty small contingent, considering how many's on the other side."

"Well, maybe we can enlarge our side some. How well do you know Frank Ellison, Jane?"

"Before the shooting that crippled him, he used to come into town quite frequently. Sometimes we'd go for rides together. Nothing romantic. But I found him interesting and enjoyed his company. This was before the silver mine reopened, of course. It was a lot quieter, and nicer, around here then."

Longarm nodded. "I got the impression you knew him pretty well when you were telling me before what happened. You seemed to be at least sympathetic with his postion."

"And I was, but that was before he unleashed Bull Denton on us."

"Jane, I think maybe you and I should take a ride out to see Frank Ellison."

"Why on earth would we do that?"

"The man's been hurt, crippled fearfully. It could explain why he's let Bull Denton run roughshod over this town. But maybe he doesn't know the worst of it."

"You mean he'll withhold his support from Denton if he finds out what Denton's been up to?"

"Yes."

"But he probably already knows every detail, and not only knows, but approves. He's a bitter, angry man, Jud. I can understand why. For someone like him to be crippled—well, it's worse than caging an eagle.

"Maybe so, Jane. I don't deny Ellison probably thinks he's got damned good reason for giving Denton a free hand. But maybe Denton has overreached himself. Maybe he's getting too greedy, even for Frank Ellison's taste. Denton has too much power, Jane, and he won't be the first man to let that unbalance him."

"Jud, why would Ellison care? He hates this town, the homesteaders, the small ranchers moving in on his grasslands."

"Don't you see it, Jane?"

She frowned. "What do you mean?"

"It won't be long now before Denton decides he's no

79

longer satisfied with only a partnership with Frank Ellison. He'll want all of Ellison's holdings. All the cattle, the land, the works."

Jane saw it at once. "Poor Frank," she said, shuddering. "He's created a monster."

"That's a good way of putting it. Now you see why I want to ride out to see Frank Ellison."

"I'll tell Andy to cut out our best saddle horses tonight and have them groomed and checked out. The chestnut for me, the black for you." She smiled for the first time in a long time. "And I'll make us a picnic basket. It'll be a long ride, Jud."

"I'll be looking forward to it."

Chapter 6

It was a little later and Longarm was in the warehouse near the loading platform, looking out at the newly repainted coach, the one Hook had stopped with his sniper fire. The workmen had done a fine job. There was no trace of the holes in the outside panel, but from what Jane had told him, they still had the upholstery to repair.

He was about to go back out through the office on his way to his hotel room when Jane came out of the office and hurried toward him.

"We've got visitors," she told him softly.

Longarm stepped to one side and glanced through a dirt-encrusted window. Slade Cullen and the Kid were strolling into the yard from the plaza, exuding an excess of mean bravado—and why not, after their triumph of the night before? Ben Blue's dry-goods store was closed for an indefinite period, Jane had told him earlier, and the storekeeper was still under the doctor's care.

The two gunslicks took their time as they glanced about them at a few of the other coaches under repair. Longarm saw the Kid open a coach door and with vicious, calculated force slam it shut again. Alongside him, a grinning Slade kicked at a wheel spoke and sent it spinning off into the yard. They were loaded for bear, eager for trouble.

And Longarm did not have to ask himself who had sent them.

"Wait a few minutes, then step out there on the platform," Longarm told Jane softly. "Find out what they want. Stall them. I don't think you'll be in any danger. They're not likely to hurt a woman."

"What are you going to do?"

"Just do as I say. Trust me."

He left Jane then, moving off through the rear of the warehouse until he came to the back door that opened out onto the yard. Stepping into the yard, he moved cautiously back along the side of the building toward the loading platform, doing his best to remain out of sight. Close to the loading platform, he peered out from behind a buggy left for repair and saw that Slade had opened the door and stepped inside the recently repaired coach. The Kid was standing back, grinning, while he held the door open for his partner. They both came alert when they saw Jane appear on the platform behind them.

"What do you two want?" she snapped angrily.

"Just having a look at this here stagecoach," the Kid said, grinning up at her. "Somebody sure made a mess of this upholstery."

As the Kid spoke, Longarm heard an extended ripping sound and knew at once that Slade, inside the coach, was ripping into the leather upholstery, finishing the job begun by Hook's two bullets. A moment later Slade stepped out of the coach, a long strip of leather dangling from his hand.

"Get out of here!" Jane cried, livid. "Both of you, or I'll—"

"Or you'll *what?*" the Kid asked eagerly. "You goin' to beat me and Slade up, are you? Now, I'd like to see that. I wouldn't mind none rasslin' with you, lady. No, I wouldn't."

"Don't start nothin' you can't finish, missy," Slade told Jane with practiced insolence. "We was told not to lay a hand on you. But that might not stop us. Sometimes we just get carried away." He chuckled then and dug the Kid with his elbow.

"You're disgusting, both of you!" Jane seethed. "Filthy degenerates, no better than that foul murderer you work for!"

"Hold your tongue, missy," Slade said, reaching out for Jane's ankle.

She jumped back, uttering a small cry. Aroused now, Slade started to boost himself up onto the loading platform.

"I wouldn't do that if I were you," Longarm said, stepping out from behind the buggy.

Slade pushed away from the platform and spun to face Longarm as his hand dropped to the six-gun on his hip, then froze. Longarm's .44 was pointed at his ample gut. Standing alongside Slade, the Kid, his hands also frozen over both six-guns, swore softly, bitterly, for having allowed himself to be taken by surprise.

Continuing toward them, Longarm said, "Drop your gun belts, both of you."

Slade complied easier than the Kid, who had to untie the rawhide strapping down both holsters. When both gun belts hit the ground, Longarm walked closer, pushed the two back almost casually, and kicked the belts well off to one side. Without looking at Jane, he told her to pick up the gun belts and leave them in the office. She jumped down lightly and a moment later disappeared into the warehouse with the guns.

"What the hell," said Slade contemptuously. "Take 'em if you want. We'll get 'em back. With maybe a little interest."

"Yeah," said the Kid, his hands on his hips, ignoring the gun in Longarm's hand. "But it'll be a cold day in hell, mister, when you ride out of this town in one piece. You just made the biggest mistake of your life."

"No," Longarm replied, "you got it backwards. You're the ones made the big mistake."

Longarm drew back his Colt and drove it as hard as he could across the Kid's face, slamming his head around with such brutal force Longarm thought he heard his neck crack. The Kid's nose disintergrated into bloody slush and his eyes rolled back in his head. He staggered back a few steps, then collapsed to the ground.

With a roar, Slade swarmed over Longarm, twisting the gun out of his hand and flinging it down, so intent was he on getting his powerful fingers around Longarm's throat. Longarm grabbed Slade's wrists and managed to pull the man's fingers away from his throat. Still holding Slade's wrists, he slammed his knee up into Slade's stomach. The man's face went white and he started to retch. Longarm stepped back from Slade. Glancing over at the Kid, he saw that, incredibly, he was beginning to stir. He stepped quickly to one side and kicked the Kid in the side of the head, flipping him over onto his back. He did not move again.

"Jud!" Jane cried from the platform. "Watch out! Slade!"

Longarm turned in time to sidestep Slade's lunging charge with relative ease, parrying Slade's wild roundhouse swings as he rushed past. Incensed out of his mind at Longarm, his fighting instincts were dulled. But as Longarm slowly circled him, waiting for his next charge, he saw the cunning return to Slade's eyes. He was, after all, an old prizefighter with skills beyond the ken of most barroom brawlers.

With a quickness that belied his bulk, Slade stepped in quickly and drove his huge right fist across Longarm's mouth. The shock of the blow went clear through Longarm, twisting him around and sending him back against the side of the stagecoach. Moving in with quick efficiency, Slade's left fist thudded against Longarm's side with rib-bending force, his right shooting out like a sledgehammer, catching Longarm square on the chin. Longarm felt himself going down.

He hit the ground shoulders first, his head reeling. Instinctively he rolled away and gathered his feet under him. He could see Slade standing over him, grinning, feet apart, doubled fists held out in front of him as they moved in a rapid milling motion. Longarm remembered Jane telling him that Slade was an ex-prizefighter, and squinting up at him now, it appeared that Slade was back in the ring, the crowd's tumultuous roar filling the air while Slade waited for this unworthy bum on the canvas before him to get back on his feet so he could pound him into insensibility.

Wiping the back of his hand across his mouth, Longarm saw the blood on it, then came up off the ground like an uncoiling spring, swinging a murderous roundhouse at Slade's grinning face. Slade sidestepped neatly, still grinning, and brought up his forearm to ward off the punch. Longarm's fist stopped into the middle of its swing, and, paying no attention to the Marquess of Queensberry's rules, he jammed his boot heel sharply into Slade's right ankle. The sudden, excruciating pain caused Slade to cry out, then automatically jerk his right leg up to grab at his ankle.

While he was thus engaged, Longarm slammed his powerful fist across the point of Slade's chin, its terrible, undeflected force knocking him backward and to the ground. Before he could roll aside, Longarm dropped onto his chest, his knees driving the breath from his lungs in a sudden, gasping exhalation. As Slade tried to suck air into his lungs, Longarm punched Slade's nose flat, smashing the bridge. Then he hit Slade repeatedly about the head and face until Slade's powerful fist pounded him in the temple, knocking him sidewise to the ground.

They both scrambled to their feet at the same time, facing each other warily, unsteadily. Seeing the groggy look in Slade's eyes and realizing he might not get another chance like this very soon, Longarm drove himself boldly at Slade, forcing him backward against the stagecoach. It was not without cost, however, as he took a sickening blow in the pit of his stomach and then a brain-rattling head punch.

But he still had Slade pinned against the side of the stagecoach and proceeded to take the man's measure, punching him with relentless precision about the face and head. Slade flung up his hefty forearms in an effort to block the punches, but Longarm drove his fists through them into Slade's face like two-by-four battering rams until at last Slade's knees began to buckle. Seeing this, his arms as heavy as railroad ties, Longarm stepped back to let Slade sag to the ground. But instead, drawing on a fierce unwillingness to go down that came from deep within his oxlike heart, Slade surged away from the stagecoach and smashed out at Longarm, his fists slashing into him with wicked, punishing force.

For a moment the two men stood trading punches, each forgetting any skill they might have learned, content to stand toe-to-toe, slugging it out. It was like a battle in some primeval forest, vicious and savage and deadly; and all Longarm could hear were his and Slade's deep grunts and the loud whacking sound of driven bone on flesh.

Longarm was aiming doggedly, relentlessly, for Slade's blood-smeared face, chopping blow after sickening blow into it, cutting Slade's lips, flattening his nose, tearing an eyebrow so badly that the blood streaming down into Slade's eyes from it nearly blinded him. Baffled, close to complete exhaustion, Slade backed up a step to get his bearings, trying to clear his vision with his own bloody fists.

Like a mountain cat scenting the kill, Longarm stepped in, his blows surer now, more savage, swifter. He hooked a left into Slade's midriff, and the bull-like figure grunted and rocked back on his heels. Again Longarm lashed out, all his weight behind a blow that struck Slade on the side of his powerful jaw. Slade's head swung around and Longarm stepped in and slashed at his head again. Slade's foot skidded out from under him and he went back heavily, coming down hard on the ground. But the man pushed himself up onto his knees and grabbed a wheel spoke and prepared to hurl it at Longarm.

Dimly, Longarm heard Jane scream, but paid no attention as he waited for Slade to fling the weapon. He did, and Longarm caught it, the weight of it sending him sprawling. Slade lunged for him. Longarm rolled over and came up, and with one wicked, cutting blow knocked Slade down onto one knee. Slade came unsteadily to his feet, his guard not yet up, and Longarm stepped coolly closer and knocked him down again with a solid, driving roundhouse.

Shaking his head, Slade shoved himself erect, and Longarm hit him again in the face, then followed this up with a second punch, and a third, each one measured with cruel precision. When Slade started to slump again, Longarm caught him by his bloodied shirtfront and held him up with his left hand while he slugged him in the face repeatedly, until Slade's head was rolling loosely on his neck and his glazed eyes were staring past Longarm.

Longarm flung the man to the ground. Slade was not quite finished yet, however. He began to crawl toward the six-gun he had knocked from Longarm's grasp earlier. Longarm stopped him with a swift kick in the midriff. The man gasped, and hugging his gut began to twist slowly, painfully, like some huge, stomped worm.

Longarm went down on one knee beside him and

leaned his face close to Slade's. "Can you hear me, Slade?"

The man's broken, swollen lips did not move, but a gleam of brute understanding flickered in his eyes.

"What you just got," Longarm told him with bitter satisfaction. "was for what you did to Ben Blue last night. How does it feel to get the shit kicked out of you, Slade?

Slade tried to say something, but all that came out of his mouth was a pink froth.

"Jud!"

Longarm looked up to see Jane jumping down from the platform. Landing like a cat, she swept up his six-gun and threw it to him. He caught the weapon, grip first.

"Hook!" she told him, pointing.

Still crouching beside Slade, Longarm swung around to see Hook stepping out from behind a coach, his rifle tucked into his shoulder. With no time to aim, Longarm snapped off a shot. The round ripped out a piece of the stagecoach inches from Hook's face. Hook ducked back behind the coach. On his feet in an instant, Longarm loped swiftly down the yard after Hook. When he reached the coach, there was no one behind it. He looked up and down the yard, but found no trace of Hook. The man had vanished like the spook he was.

Jane sent Fred over to the Silverado to find Denton and tell him to send someone for Slade and the Kid, who was now conscious, but totally disoriented. When three of Denton's gunslicks came running and hauled off the two, she went upstairs where Longarm was already

89

slumped wearily at the kitchen table, sipping coffee he had managed to heat up.

Jane went promptly to work on the weary gladiator, washing off his face first of all, wincing when he winced, her hands gentle, yet sure. While she worked, Tomlinson came into the kitchen to hear the details. His eyes were glowing when Jane finished, the news of what Longarm had done to Denton's two bullyboys putting new life into him.

Jane dipped her towel in the icy water, wrung it out, and pressed it against Longarm's mouth, his forehead, and the back of his neck. She had already used barely moisturized soap to stop the bleeding from a cut at the corner of his mouth. One of Longarm's eyes was swollen, but he could see out of it well enough. And there was a gash on his forehead close to the hairline. Meanwhile, Longarm's upper arms, shoulders, and belly were throbbing steadily. He felt as if he had gotten caught up in a waterwheel and gone around too many times.

With the wet towel still draped over the back of his neck, Jane helped Longarm take off his brown tweed frock coat. It was torn in several places and the right sleeve had been ripped from its socket. But Jane assured him she would mend it that evening, and that after a good cleaning, the coat would be as good as new.

Feeling better, Longarm let her have the coat and took the damp towel from around his neck.

"What're you going to do now?" Tomlinson asked him.

"Go over to my hotel and get some fresh duds. Why?"

"Why? Good God, man! You sure as hell must know

by now what Denton does to them that messes with his gunslicks. He ain't goin' to be very happy with what you just done to his two pets."

"No, I don't suppose he is."

"So what're you going to do?" Tomlinson asked again.

"Yes, Jud," Jane seconded, frowning with concern. "Maybe you'd better keep low for a while."

Longarm got up from the table. "First things first," he told them. "Right now I need a little shut-eye and some clean duds." Then he looked directly at Jane. "And don't forget to pack that picnic basket for tomorrow's ride out to Frank Ellison's place."

Carefully, he set his hat down onto his battered head; then, with a casual wave, he buttoned his vest and strode from the kitchen, the cross-draw rig holding his Colt .44 clearly visible if any of Denton's men wanted to stop him.

He reached his hotel room without incident, flung off his dusty, dirt-smeared pants, and stepped into a gray pair. Pulling a fresh white broadcloth shirt out of his carpetbag, he put it on, then shrugged into a wrinkled frock coat that at least matched his pants. Buckling on his cross-draw rig, he set his hat back on his head and left the room, flexing both hands to keep his fingers from stiffening up. His bruised knuckles made just moving them a painful ordeal.

As he pushed through the Silverado's doors a few minutes later, he did not go unnoticed. There was a subtle but noticeable drop in the level of conversation, and every stride he took toward the bar caused the sound level to decrease still further. Longarm bellied up to the bar and shucked his hat off his forehead. The barkeep finished wiping off a section of the bar before he moved over to serve Longarm.

"Maryland rye," Longarm said.

"You been in here before, mister," the barkeep told him, savoring the moment as everyone in the hushed saloon listened to each word. He was a big man with thinning black hair slicked straight back, and a sweeping, meticulously oiled mustache. "You know we don't carry that sheep dip in here. It ain' fit for a snake to drink."

"Well, fine then," Longarm said genially. "Any good whiskey you might recommend would be fine."

This momentarily stymied the barkeep. He had been trying to curry favor with his boss by putting Longarm in his place. Like everyone in there, he had heard by now what Longarm had done to Slade and the Kid. The barkeep recovered quickly, however, and took an unlabeled bottle from under the counter and poured Longarm a shot.

"That'll be four bits," he said, as Longarm reached for the glass. The barkeep knew and Longarm knew that such an amount for a single shot was outrageous.

Longarm dropped a silver coin on the bar that would more than cover it, lifted the shot glass to his lips, and tipped his head back. He let none of it go down, however, but swished it around in his mouth. As he had suspected, it was pure kerosene, what the man used to fill the wall lamps behind him.

Longarm pretended to swallow the whiskey, slapped the glass back down on the counter, and pushed it toward the barkeep. As the man, vastly amused, poured another shot, Longarm blew the kerosene he had kept in his mouth into the barkeep's face, then dashed the contents of the bottle after it. In a moment a match was in his hand, his thumb flicking it to life. Before the bartender could duck back, Longarm tossed the match at the man. Immediately, his hair caught. With a scream the barkeep turned and ran down the length of the bar, beating frantically at the flames on his shirtfront and the left side of his face.

Longarm looked coolly at another barkeep farther down. The man's hands were under the counter, groping for the shotgun, Longarm knew. Longarm took out his Colt and leveled it at the man.

"Put your hands on the bar where I can see them."

The barkeep did as he was told.

"Now, come on out here."

Moving with surprising alacrity for a man of his heft, the barkeep hustled out from behind the bar. As he did so, Longarm moved down the bar until he was directly under the armed guard on the balcony. Swiftly, he moved close against the wall.

All this had happened so quickly, the man had not had time to lever a cartridge into his firing chamber, and now Longarm was out of sight under him. Longarm heard the guard scramble from his chair and pound off down the balcony—heading for Denton, Longarm had no doubt.

The other two guards, caught flat-footed amidst the crowd of transfixed patrons, were watching Longarm warily, apparently trying to decide whether or not they should lift their rifles and trade shots with him.

Longarm looked at them both and shook his head.

"Why get yourself all shot up for no reason?" he asked mildly. "I just came in here to see your boss, that's all. No need to get riled. Why don't you just put them carbines aside, gents."

Without a word, the two men carefully stepped forward to place their carbines down on the table in front of them.

As the carbines clattered to rest, there came from the balcony above the sound of hurrying feet, and then Denton could be seen plunging down the stairs, the Kid on his heels. The Kid did not look at all good. The side of his face was swollen where Longarm had kicked him, and his nose was a bloody, scabbed-over mess. When his eyes lit on Longarm, his hands dropped eagerly to his holsters.

"I wouldn't do that, Kid," Longarm barked, raising his Colt idly. "You'll only be putting you boss in the line of fire. Not to mention all these patrons."

"Dammit, Kid!" Denton cried, slapping the Kid's right hand away from his side arm. "Not here. Not now. you had your chance and blew it."

The Kid took a deep, miserable breath, and backed off. Denton strode across the saloon to Longarm. "You come in here for trouble, Drake?"

"I came in to see you, as a matter of fact. I thought we had a business deal to discuss. But your barkeep tried to poison me."

"So you set him afire."

"That's what you do with kerosene when you can't drink it."

"He was a fool. Come upstairs."

Longarm followed Denton into his office and slumped in his leather armchair and took out a cheroot. Denton closed the door and moved around behind his desk. When Longarm offered him a cheroot, Denton shook his head. His gaze was cold, calculating. And something else.

"Mr. Drake," he said, shifting back in his swivel chair, "you are a difficult man to figure. There's more to you than meets the eye. Before we conclude any deals, maybe you better tell me something about yourself."

"Nothing much to tell. Came here with a stake. Figured I might buy into a saloon or a hotel. I'm a gambler by profession."

"And a gunman, too, I'll wager."

"In my business a man has to know how to defend himself."

"Yes, he does. And you seem to know how to do that. Slade Cullen is not an easy man to club insensible with bare fists, but you managed that, and you look barely winded."

Longarm shrugged.

"If I were you, I'd watch out for the Kid, though. He means to have your ass."

"Tell him he's welcome to try. Any time."

Denton tipped his head and studied Longarm coldly for a moment. "And I do believe you mean that."

"Just how much will it cost the line for you to call off your dogs and give the stage protection from Indians, highwaymen, and other undesirables?"

"Before I tell you, I want to know why you're getting involved in this."

"What's so hard for you to understand? This stage line looks like a fine investment. And a lot safer than gambling for a living. That is, if you're serious about granting us that protection."

"I am. But for a price, and you know what that price is."

"Thirty percent is pretty steep."

"It's thirty percent or nothing."

"Let's think on that a moment," Longarm suggested, taking his cheroot from his mouth and leaning forward in his chair. "Why not make it twenty-five percent for you, and five percent for me."

"Why should I cut you in for five percent?"

"Because I'm going to make sure you have no more trouble with Tomlinson and his daughter. I'll see to it, also, that the stage line keeps running and that your percentage is always paid on time."

"I thought you were on their side."

"I'm on my side, Denton. Always my side. Soon enough I'll get my original investment back, and then some. This way, we're both happy. Me, I'm getting my investment back under the table, and you're getting a healthy bit of extortion."

Denton frowned, seriously considering the proposal. "Well, now, I don't know," he said, his brows knitting. "I sure as hell wasn't planning on letting you in on this."

"Oh, for Christ's sake, Denton, don't be so greedy."

Denton was about to snap back at Longarm. He wasn't used to having anyone talk to him in that tone. But he shook off his irritation, thought a moment longer, then came out from behind his desk and shot out his hand.

"It's a deal, Drake."

The two men shook on it.

"One more thing, Denton."

"What's that?"

"Keep Hook off my back. If he comes snooping after me with that new rifle of his, I'll kill the son of a bitch."

"I'll tell him. But I ain't promisin' anything. He has a mind of his own about some things."

"Just tell him what I said, then."

"Sure."

Longarm got to his feet. "I'm sure we can work out the details later. But the next time I come into your establishment for a drink, I hope your barkeep will be more hospitable. Maybe you can talk him into stocking some Maryland rye."

"I'll see to it."

Longarm left.

As he descended the stairs and strode through the suddenly quiet saloon, Hook—having just entered and taken his favorite table in the rear—stubbed out his cigar and reached for his rifle. He thought Longarm might have caught a glimpse of him, but that hardly mattered.

As soon as Longarm pushed through the batwings, Hook got up and followed out of the Silverado after him. Keeping in the shadows, he watched the tall man stride toward his hotel a few blocks down. When Longarm entered, Hook took a position in the entrance to an alley across from the hotel and waited. If it became clear that Longarm had retired for the night, Hook would simply wait until he was sure the man was asleep, then visit him in his room and finish him quietly with his bowie. The son of a bitch's scalp would be a happy surprise for Denton, he was sure.

When Longarm came out a moment later and ducked swiftly into the alley beside the hotel, Hook was pleased. If there was one thing he liked, it was a chase. He darted from the shadowed storefront, slipped into the alley, and followed after Longarm, keeping close to the building's shadow. His boots made no sound on the hard-packed, rutted alley. Longarm reached the other end of the alley and turned onto a narrow back street.

Hook halted. He knew an ambush when he saw one. Changing course, he crossed the alley, cut behind a feed-and-grain store, and kept going on around it until he reached the street down which Longarm had cut. He cocked his rifle and shifted it to his left hand. With his right hand, he reached back and drew his knife from its sheath, then moved cautiously down the dark street, crossing in front of dark storefronts and low porches fronting parlor houses. Not until he had gone three blocks did he catch sight of Longarm strolling along nonchalantly ahead of him.

Feeling a little foolish, Hook increased his pace until he was within a block of his quarry. Abruptly, Longarm turned in to an alley. This time Hook didn't take the bait. He cut behind a house and found a narrow alley that paralleled the side street, intersecting the alley farther down, and hurried along it.

When he broke out into the alley, his eyes, well adjusted to the dark by then, caught an ominous shape crouched down on the other side of the alley, a rifle laid across a rain barrel, its muzzle facing the street. Had Hook followed Longarm, he would have been blasted the moment he appeared in the mouth of the alley. He swore softly. He had not seen the rifle in Longarm's possession, but he knew it could have been slipped down inside his pants and in the dark not have been noticed. He shuddered. This was no ordinary man, he was beginning to realize.

Still, it was Hook's advantage now.

Slipping across the alley and flattening himself

against a wall, Hook paused, studying Longarm's crouched figure. The rifle had not wavered since Hook first spotted it, which meant Longarm had not seen him dart across the alley behind him and was still expecting him to appear at the head of the alley. That meant Hook had to move swiftly, before the gambler got suspicious and started looking around.

Crouching low, his knife out and gleaming in the dim light, Hook swept swiftly, silently, through the darkness toward Longarm's crouched figure. Just behind Longarm, Hook's eyes struggled with the form of the creature before him, trying to make sense of it—and then he realized he was looking not at a man crouching behind the barrel, but at a dark blanket thrown over a series of wooden boxes.

As for the rifle, it had been propped atop the barrel and left there. He jumped forward, kicked the empty boxes aside, and snatched at it, recognizing it instantly as the same rifle he had lost outside the canyon. His fingers explored the stock and found where the bullet had entered and still remained.

Sheathing his knife and placing his new rifle against the wall, he let his fingers play over his old weapon. Denton had been right. Hook had put great store by this rifle. He hefted it, and checking the load, realized it was already loaded.

Had Longarm been prepared to use it on him, then lost his nerve?

Lugging both rifles, he headed across town toward his own room in back of the barbershop. Once inside he threw his new rifle to one side, lit a lamp, and examined more closely the rifle Longarm had returned to him.

Outside of the slug embedded in the stock, it still

seemed in excellent condition. Hook went on examining the rifle, his elation building. Was this fellow bargaining for a truce of some kind? Turning the lamp up still more, he opened the chamber mechanism. Everything was in fine working order, the smell of machine oil fresh and familiar. He raised the rifle to the lamp and looked down the barrel.

A chunk of lead was stuck halfway down the barrel.

It had been jammed in there so securely it could not be rammed out without ruining the rifling inside the barrel. And if Hook had tried to fire it before checking it out, it would have blown up in his face.

Damn, Hook thought with grudging admiration, this man plays dangerous games.

Chapter 7

In the stage office the next morning, before he rode out with Jane, Longarm told her, Tomlinson, and Jimmy Hunnicut of the "deal" he had made the night before with Denton. They'd already heard about his run-in with the Silverado barkeep. When Longarm finished his account of his meeting with Denton, Tomlinson chuckled and shook his head in pure admiration.

"I'm sure glad you're an honest man, Drake," he drawled, nudging Jane. "Otherwise we wouldn't have a chance—not against Denton *and* you."

"Stop it, Dad," Jane said. Then she peered hopefully at Longarm. "Do you think this deal will satisfy Denton?"

"For now. And it'll keep Hook from throwing any more lead at your stagecoaches while we prepare our surprise for Denton."

"What surprise?" Hunnicut asked.

"Jane and I are riding out now to fashion it," Longarm told him.

"Never mind, boy," Tomlinson said to Hunnicut. "I'll fill you in. Drake told me all about it, and what he's got in mind is just crazy enough to work. One way or the other, we'll flush a whole mess of cockroaches out of the woodwork."

Jane looked at her father. "Is Jimmy still living in the hotel room?"

"No. I figure he'll be safer bunkin' in with the drivers. He'll be keeping his hind end down until we make our move." Tomlinson looked at Longarm. "You take good care of this daughter of mine, Drake."

"I'll do my best," Longarm replied. Then he turned to Jane. "Ready to move out?"

"The horses are waiting," Jane said suddenly, her eyes glowing. She picked up the saddlebag she had filled with food. When she saw the surprise on Longarm's face at the sight of the bulging saddlebag, she smiled at him. "There's plenty in there. Don't worry. But there's no place for a picnic basket on a horse."

"That'll do fine," Longarm said as the four of them filed out of the office and walked over to the stables. Andy had their horses already out of their stalls and saddled, bedrolls and camping gear tied on behind the cantles. It looked like the old wrangler had already given the horses a good currying. Jane gave Andy the saddlebags to tie on, and took the reins from him.

Longarm stood back to watch. From the moment he first caught sight of her that morning, Longarm had been finding it difficult to keep his eyes off her. She would not be riding sidesaddle and had dressed accordingly, in Levi's, a man's blue cotton shirt with sleeves rolled up, and a black, flat-crowned sombrero. About her throat she had knotted a bright blue bandanna. She was wearing men's clothing, all right, but it sure as hell didn't make her look like a man, especially when she pulled herself up into the saddle and Longarm caught the generous swell of her breasts thrusting boldly against her cotton shirt.

As Jane pulled her chestnut around, Longarm swung up onto the black, and with a wave to the others, followed Jane out of the stable yard and headed out of the quiet, still-sleeping town.

They headed west, following the route Longarm had taken earlier when he had ridden into the hills shimmering now in the distance. Once they reached the grasslands, Jane took over, following a rising trail that curved and twisted between steep, thickly timbered slopes. They climbed steadily through the morning, riding single file in the timber, Jane in the lead. At midday they found an open park fed by a seep. Here they let their horses graze while they ate the sandwiches Jane had prepared.

The picnic lunch eaten, Jane stretched out on the grass and before long was asleep. Watching her, Longarm found himself wondering what was ahead for the two of them when this was all over. Jane was a very pretty, vibrant young lady, and Longarm could feel himself being drawn to her. Once he got Hook, his mission would be accomplished and any interest in Jane—or her stage line—would have to be put behind him as he returned to Denver for that bonus he had been promised.

If he wanted to return, that is.

Without the mantle of the federal government to direct his actions, a badge to flash and proper warrants to follow, he found himself moving in ways and in directions that intrigued him. He liked enormously this new freedom of action it gave him, without the nagging restraints that working on a case as a deputy U.S. marshal sometimes demanded.

Jane awakened and turned her head to look at him.

"I must have dozed off," she said.

"Good for you. We covered a lot of ground this morning."

"Yes," she said, getting up and walking over to him. She stood between him and the sun for a moment, then dropped beside him and plucked a grass stem to chew on. "Aren't you sleepy?"

"It's not sleep I need."

"Oh, what is it you need?" Longarm could tell from the impish gleam in her eyes that she knew perfectly well.

For an answer, he reached out and slowly unbuttoned her shirt. She did nothing to stop him. Instead, she undid her hair and let her long chestnut curls spill luxuriantly down over her shoulders. As he had suspected, she wore no corset under her shirt, and when he peeled it back off her, she was bare to the waist, her melon-shaped breasts glowing. He let both hands fall gently upon them, their incredible warmth flowing through them, clear to his groin. He pressed her down on the grass and took first one nipple and then the other gently in his mouth until both were as hard as bullets—and she was feverishly unbuckling her Levi's.

After kicking off his boots, Longarm used one hand to slip out of his pants and drawers, and almost before either of them knew it, he was lying between her thighs, her tight buttocks rising to accommodate his entry, which happened so easily, he was hardly aware of it.

For them both it had been a long wait and—as was perfectly plain to Longarm—it was something both had been hungering for from the moment they first met. His knees digging into the soft ground, he leaned forward urgently and found himself thrusting eagerly, his need boiling up from his groin, impaling her on his fiery tip. Jane's head began flipping from side to side, her face flushing, her tongue sliding back and forth across her upper lip. His urgent thrusting seemed to rock the cool, fragrant ground beneath him as her urgent pleading for him to go faster, deeper, gave way to sharp outcries, and their entwined, heaving bodies became welded to the earth under them, and to the blue sky arching overhead. In this pagan embrace they were animals like any others, copulating under the sun's warm benevolence in triumphant celebration of their youth and vigor.

As he climaxed, she tightened her vaginal muscles about him, and he felt her trembling wildly under him, her arms encircling his neck, momentarily threatening to cut off his breathing as she came also. Again and again she climaxed, the intensity dying only slowly.

When she was done, he started to release her.

"No, no!" she cried, sucking him in. "Not so soon. It's been so long."

He wanted to protest. He was spent. The next time he would be more thoughtful, would move slower and with less urgency, and then it would not be over so soon. But he said nothing and let her pull him deeper into her lush, moist warmth. He heard her sigh and was content.

Still lying within her thighs, he almost slept, his

naked chest resting upon the soft, incandescent warmth of her breasts, his head cradled between her shoulder and head, deep in the fragrant opulence of her chestnut curls. What awakened him was the sense of his loins quickening, the sudden awareness of a renewed urgency. He felt her move slowly, lasciviously under him, the insides of her thighs pressing against the outsides of his, her hot breath on his earlobe. He lifted his head. Her eyes were closed, but she was waiting. He kissed her on the lips, his tongue thrusting past her moist, pliant lips, and felt her own deliciously wanton, probing tongue greet his in response.

Now it was her turn, and she proceeded to work her will on him. She went at her own speed, slowly at first, but increasing the tempo with maddening effectiveness, following an intoxicating rhythm that was soon sweeping him along. She had an abundance of tricks, each one more maddening than the last. At first she was on top, teasing him almost to a climax. Then she maneuvered him to one side, her wild, finely controlled passion sweeping him along with her. When at last she allowed them to be caught up in what they could no longer control, and they had both expended their final, thrusting urgency, the real world swam into focus around them, and she unclasped him, smiling, and rolled onto her side. This time she did not protest his withdrawal.

He was spent completely, his loins gutted. The world about him seemed to sparkle, as if it had just been minted, and he knew he had just had a very good time, one that would not leave him with a headache the next morning or a sour taste in his mouth.

Propped up on her elbow, still naked, Jane plucked

another long grass stem and began chewing on it. She glowed with health. Her eyes were bright and clear, her cheeks rosy.

"At this rate," she reminded him impishly, "we're not going to reach Ellison's ranch today."

"I wasn't planning to go there directly, anyway."

"Oh?"

"I'd like to see the extent of his range, or as near as you can show me in a couple of extra days."

"Why?"

"If what I got in mind is going to succeed, I'll have to know this country's layout."

"And just what might you have in mind?"

He smiled. "I'll tell you later, after we get a chance to talk to Ellison. A lot depends on his reaction to what we tell him. The thing is, does he trust you? Will he believe you?"

"Yes, he will, Jud. I'm sure of it."

"Good. Now let's put ourselves back together, before we catch a chill."

She laughed and rolled onto her back, stretching her arms out. "I'm not in much danger of that, Jud. It's so nice like this—I mean the feel of the warm sun on me. All of me. A woman doesn't get many chances to do this, you know."

He looked at her, savoring the hills and valleys, the swells and dips of her long, lithe body. It was true what she said—that a woman didn't get the chance to lie naked in the sun like this—and that was a shame, sure enough.

He reached out for one of those swelling hills.

• • •

107

On the morning of the third day after leaving Sand Hills, they cut onto the rutted trace leading to Ellison's ranch and followed it for about five miles until they reached the Circle D compound. It was at the end of a long, grassy valley.

By this time, Longarm had seen enough of the surrounding country to know how he was going to operate through it when the time came. He had also had a good look at Bull Denton's smaller spread, one that Denton had only recently purchased, according to what Jane had heard. Overtaking some of Denton's cattle along the way, he noted the brand Denton had adopted. In the shape of a spoked wheel, it was of more than passing interest in light of Frank Ellison's Circle D brand, with its circle forming the back of the *D*. Any rider with an educated running iron would not have to work very hard to transform Ellison's brand to a near-perfect duplicate of Denton's.

Frank Ellison's main house was a rambling adobe structure with a tile roof and a long portico that ran the length of it. Horse barns, a bunkhouse, blacksmith shed, and other outbuildings fanned out behind it toward a large corral. As Longarm and Jane dismounted in front of the house, Frank Ellison came hobbling out onto the porch on crutches, greeting Jane heartily, inviting them both in with what Longarm felt at once was a hearty, almost eager pleasure in the prospect of their company.

In the portico's blessed shade, Jane introduced Longarm. Shaking Ellison's hand, Longarm found his grasp amazingly strong. The man's strength and vigor were also apparent in his thick crown of white hair, his massive brow, and solid, powerful shoulders. His penetrating gaze reminded Longarm of Jane's reference to him as a caged eagle. It was more than apt. Though Ellison was not the kind of man who would complain of any discomfort, the lines in his face indicated a constant, draining pain, and Longarm could not help noticing how uselessly the man's right leg dangled as he lunged forward on his crutches and ushered them into the house.

A pretty Zuni housekeeper, not much older than thirty, appeared as if by magic before them, and Ellison told her there would be two guests for the noon meal. A wiry young Zuni lad, bearing a remarkable resemblance to both Ellison and his Zuni housekeeper, appeared next and was sent to fetch the foreman and then see to Jane's and Longarm's horses.

As Ellison eased into an upholstered armchair in the cool, spacious living room, Jane and Longarm sat back on a leather sofa. A moment later the Zuni woman brought them tall, cool glasses of lemonade. Soon they were joined by Ellison's foreman, Pablo Sanchez. He was a tall, swarthy man with gleaming black hair and a meticulously oiled mustache. There was more Spanish blood in him than Indian, but as he eased his long-shanked body into a wooden rocker beside Ellison and gazed into Longarm's eyes, Longarm saw more Indian than Spanish blood looking out at him.

After a few light preliminary remarks, during which Jane took the opportunity to explain that Longarm was thinking of buying into their stage line, Ellison remarked with a smile that he knew the two of them had not ridden out this far for lemonade and dinner.

Jane spoke up promptly. "You're right, Frank. Though it was a nice ride, and I won't say your hospitality is not worth it."

"You are very kind. Now, tell me. Why have you come?"

"There's been trouble in town, Frank," she told him bluntly. "Bad trouble."

"Oh?'

"And your partner Bull Denton is responsible."

"How so, Jane?"

"He's the only law in Sand Hills, Frank. But he's an outlaw."

"I'm sorry to hear you say that, Jane. But there's nothing I can do. I gave him a free hand, and I intend to see that he keeps it. I've had enough of those townsmen and their brand of justice. Now they'll get a taste of mine."

"Including a lynching?"

Ellison frowned. "Would you care to explain that?"

Jane did, sparing the man no details, and when she had finished, a slightly shaken Ellison glanced quickly at his foreman. "You heard about this?"

"Some of the men were talking about it," admitted Sanchez. "I was going to mention it."

Ellison looked back at Jane. "I must admit, that is not pleasant news. I knew Dean Clairborn. I liked him. It must be very bad for his widow."

"There's more, Frank."

"Go on."

"Denton's brought in a killer. He dresses in black and he keeps himself hidden for the most part. But he shot down two of our horses, stopping one of our stages. He put two bullets through the side panel. Then he shot Dad."

"Your father? My God, how is he?"

"He's up and around now. Jud here was on the stage

110

and went after the sniper. That's the only reason I can see why Denton's killer didn't finish Dad off."

Ellison looked hard at Longarm. "Are you sure this man Denton brought in was the one firing on you?"

"Yes."

Ellison looked back at Jane. "You have my word, Jane. I knew nothing about this man. But what possible reason would he have for shooting up the stage and firing on your father?"

"He's putting pressure on us to sell him the stage line. Right now, he's made a deal, through Jud here, to lay off us. All we have to do is give him thirty percent of our profits."

Ellison's bushy eyebrows shot up in surprise. "Did you say thirty percent?"

"Yes."

"And you're going to pay it?"

"Not if we can help it," Longarm drawled, smiling.

Ellison looked at Longarm and then back at Jane. "I see," he said, after a long pause. "You want me to see what I can do to curb Denton."

"No. Not curb him. I want you to disavow him. Buy him out and tell him he's finished."

Wearily, Ellison shook his head. "Bull Denton's my partner. I need him. That damned rustler left me a cripple. I can get around in a spring wagon or a buggy, but I can no longer ride. Denton's my eyes and ears now. He's taking care of our investments in town, and since he's joined me, there's been an end to the rustling that was cutting me in half. In addition, not a single nester has sunk a plow into my grasslands. I tried the law and it didn't work. They set free the man who crippled me. If Denton's tough on the townsmen and nesters, and those two-bit ranchers who were nibbling away at my herds, that's just fine with me."

"Is that your final word, Frank?" Jane asked.

"No, Jane, it isn't. I'll pay for your new horses and for the repairs to your stage. I'll give word to the bank to advance you whatever it costs from my account. And I'll tell Denton to forget that extortion. You won't have to pay him any thirty percent. I'll see to that."

"That's very generous of you, Frank. And I certainly appreciate it. But does that mean you won't stop Bull Denton?"

"I've just told you why I can't do that."

"Not even to save your own ranch?" Longarm suggested quietly.

Ellison swiveled to face Longarm. "Now, just what do you mean by that?"

"How do you know he won't turn on you? He's greedy enough. He's got the men, a small army. How many riders do you have?"

"Twelve, not including Sanchez here."

"Well, Denton has as many, and his riders are ruthless gunslicks, not a working cowhand among them. How do you think your hands would do facing that kind of an opposition?"

"You're trying to turn me against my partner," Ellison snapped, viewing Longarm with undisguised hostility. Jane he could be patient with, but not Longarm, whom he obviously regarded as an interloper.

"I'm just saying," Longarm continued quietly, "that the more you feed Bull Denton, the more his appetite will grow. I've seen it before. A man as greedy as Bull Denton never knows where to stop."

"Maybe so, but he knows which side his bread is buttered on."

"For now, maybe. But think a minute. How can you keep track of him? You can't really. And he knows that. Denton's got a spread between here and town, hasn't he?"

"He has."

"Before long, some of your cattle will be missing again. Denton will make a big show of going after those responsible. He'll maybe even drag in a few homesteaders to convince you he's doing his job. But you'll go right on missing cattle."

"And his own herds," said Jane, "will keep on growing."

"He's too smart to try anything like that on me," Ellison insisted. "And besides, I'll have Sanchez here to keep an eye on him."

Sanchez cleared his throat nervously. "Frank," he said, "I been noticing that wagon wheel brand Denton's using. It's awful damn close to ours."

"Are we losing any cattle? Have you seen any evidence of him tampering with the brands on our stock?"

"Nope."

Ellison turned back to Jane and Longarm. "I'm not kidding myself. Don't think I am. Bull Denton is a ruthless and greedy man. But he knows enough not to go against me. I have powerful backers in Santa Fe. My money put most of them there in the first place, and the governor is a personal friend. Without my backing, Denton would be nothing in this territory, and he knows that."

Jane sighed and changed the subject. At once the tension in the room lifted, and Frank Ellison proved he

113

could be a charming host. He had known Kit Carson and even ridden with him in '64, when he rounded up the Mescalero Apaches and Navahos and confined them to the Bosque Redondo agency. With this as his background, he had many rousing tales to tell, which he did all through the superb dinner his Zuni housekeeper prepared.

Declining Ellison's offer to stay the night, Longarm and Jane rode out that afternoon. Jane was discouraged. As far as she was concerned, the long trip had accomplished little. Though Ellison had assured her he would pay for the two horses and the damage to their stagecoach, she had not ridden out there for that. And she had little faith that Denton could be persuaded by Ellison to halt his extortion of their line.

"Cheer up," Longarm told her. "We did accomplish one thing."

"And what was that?"

"We planted a seed."

She tipped her head. "I'm listening."

"A seed of distrust. Already Ellison's foreman is thinking about that brand Denton is using. And the likelihood of Circle D cattle being rustled by Denton has been planted securely in Ellison's thinking."

"What good does that do?"

"When Denton does start rustling Circle D cattle and changing their brands, he will have gone too far. Then Ellison will turn on him with his own men. Denton will be finished."

"But supposing Denton doesn't start rustling Frank's cattle?"

"Oh, he will—and soon."

"Now, how on earth would you know that?"

Longarm glanced at her, a sly grin on his face. "I just got this feeling."

Chapter 8

Longarm lay motionless in the darkness, his Winchester in the grass beside him. He had been perched on this ridge for some time, his eyes on the line shack below him. Lost in the night shadow under the big fir, his prone body was invisible to anyone more than ten yards distant.

The line shack was deep in the mountains north of Ellison's ranch. A place for a pair of line riders to put up for the night while they spent their days combing the narrow canyons and draws for straying Circle D cattle. When Longarm had passed by this cabin with Jane, he'd had a chance to study it pretty thoroughly, the line shack and the country around. There was a similar line shack farther east.

Longarm glanced behind him into a shallow pocket below the ridge. A small fire had been built in the pocket, one just hot enough to heat a branding iron. Alongside its flickering glow, Tomlinson's bent figure was in the act of drawing his white-hot running iron from the fire's core. Behind him, Hunnicut was holding down a roped steer. Longarm turned his attention back to the line shack below him.

The steer bawled out loudly as Tomlinson's hot running iron seared its hide, its protest loud enough to carry far. Those two Circle D riders in the line shack below him must be sleeping mighty sound, Longarm reflected. This was not the first steer to let out such a frantic bleat. Longarm decided Ellison's riders had gotten too soft, now that Denton had succeeded in chasing away the rustlers that once pillaged Circle D herds.

The cabin door swung wide and a shadowy figure stepped into the doorway, his head cocked, listening. The bright wash of moonlight enabled Longarm to see that the line rider was standing in his long johns, a rifle in his hand.

Longarm had already levered a cartridge into his Winchester's firing chamber. He tucked its stock into his shoulder, aimed at the man, lifted the rifle a fraction, and pulled off a shot. The bullet smacked into the doorjamb over the man's head. He jumped back inside and slammed the door shut. Longarm cranked a new shell into place and fired again, this time sending a round into the top log framing the window. He waited for the line riders' reaction.

Not that he expected any return fire from the cabin. What would the two line riders be shooting at? If they were smart, they would be flat on the floor now, cursing, wondering who in hell was firing at them in the middle of the night, and why. Thinking this, Longarm chuckled and sent a round through the window, the sound of its spraying glass shards filling the night.

This final shot was calculated to keep them on the floor until morning at least.

And when they did emerge from the line shack, guns out and ready, expecting the worst, they would find that three of their four horses were gone, leaving only one man able to ride to the Circle D for help.

Longarm waited, his finger resting against the Winchester's trigger. But as he had assumed, no shots came from the line shack, nor any outcry from within demanding an explanation for this sudden warfare, as the two line riders kept their asses down. Tomlinson materialized out of the night and crouched down beside Longarm. He was moving a lot slower than would have been the case had he not been shot a week before, but he was getting around well enough.

"Them two still in there?" he asked.

Longarm nodded. "And they'll stay there, until morning, at least."

"You sure of that?"

"Wait a minute and I'll make sure."

Longarm lifted the Winchester and put two rounds into the stovepipe chimney, sending it clattering off the roof.

Then he followed Tomlinson to the bottom of the slope where Hunnicut waited astride his mount. He had already doused the fire, mixing its ashes with dirt and scattering them carefully over the grass. The last steer they had used the running iron on could still be heard plunging off into the brush after the others. It would be well into the morning before searching Circle D riders would come upon them, noting at once the fresh new brands seared on their hides.

Bull Denton's wagon wheel brand.

They rode for a quarter of a mile, through winding ravines and steep-sided draws, coming at last to the three horses they had taken from the line shack. Dismounting beside them, they tied already prepared, rock-filled aparejos to their backs, then mounted up and rode on, each rider leading a horse.

Splashing through a shallow creek not much later, Longarm looked back. In the moonlight he could see the tracks left by all six horses as they climbed the soft bank. They were deep enough, indicating that each horse was carrying the weight of a rider. Six mounted and armed rustlers made a formidable group to tackle, and with this in mind any riders coming after them would go about it with great care, perhaps even reluctance.

Satisfied, Longarm turned back around and led his fellow rustlers on through the rough country to a small clearing where they had left the thirty head of cattle they had gathered earlier. Hazing them into a bunch, they drove them deeper into the mountains, leaving a trail the poorest tracker could follow.

They kept the herd moving for over an hour until they entered a large patch of timber. With the trees breaking up the gather, all the men had to do was keep hazing them on until the cattle had vanished into the woods, pounding off in different directions. It would take Ellison's riders one hell of a long time to comb all those cattle out of the timber.

Longarm then led Tomlinson and Hunnicut east, on his way to the other Circle D line shack. He figured to get there a little before dawn, which exactly suited his purpose.

With the first light of dawn the two punchers in the eastern line shack came awake. They turned out of their bunks and pulled on their boots without a word to each other. They made an odd pair. One was a raw kid just turned seventeen. The other was an old stove-up cowpuncher, kept on because Ellison had known the cowpuncher in better days. His name was Pete. No one knew what the rest of it was, and Pete was not telling. Now, sitting up on his bunk and scratching his head, he glared blearily about him, unable to function, as usual, without his first cup of scalding-hot coffee.

The kid knew this by now and hurried from the cabin with a bucket to get fresh water from the stream. Seeing this, Pete roused himself and began shoving firewood into the stove. Before Pete could get the firewood blasing, the kid was back. With an empty bucket.

"Where the hell's the water?" Pete demanded.

"I didn't get any."

"Why in hell not?"

"Two of our horses are gone."

"Gone? You mean they strayed off?"

"Hell, no! They was taken, Pete!"

"Oh, shit," the old cowpoke said, reaching for his gun belt.

In a moment, guns strapped to their waists and Pete lugging a rifle, they hurried out and saddled up the remaining two mounts, then rode off after the stolen horses.

The tracks of the missing pair were easy to follow. So were the bootprints left by the man on foot who had led them away. After a stretch the bootprints stopped, and from then on their horses were driven off by a horse and rider. The tracks led up into a country of high peaks slashed by narrow canyons and deep, twisting gorges.

A mile or so farther on, the stolen horses disappeared into a stretch of heavy timber. Pete and the kid kept on, but couldn't find the tracks when they reached the other side of the timber. What they came on instead were the hoofprints of over fifty head of cattle heading east.

Pete pulled his mount to a halt and stared bleakly at the tracks left by the herd. The kid glanced over at him uncertainly.

"Rustlers?"

"You're goddamned right it's rustlers," Pete snapped. "Cattle don't bunch up like that and head away from water and fresh graze unless they're driven. You have a look over there on the right. I want to know how many rustlers we got to deal with here."

As the kid trotted off, Pete dismounted and studied the ground carefully. Then he got back into his saddle and nudged his horse along for a little ways, studying the ground carefully all the while.

"I got three mounted riders on this side!" the kid called, lifting his horse to a lope as he rode back toward Pete.

"And I make out five more on this side," Pete growled unhappily as the kid pulled alongside of him. "That makes eight riders, all told."

"Christ, Pete, that's a helluva lot for us to mess with, ain't it?"

"You're goddamned right it is. Come on, we're riding back to the ranch—fast."

The two men wheeled their horses and headed for the Circle D.

Longarm was sick of eating dust, and he was sure Tomlinson and Hunnicut felt the same way, but there was no way to avoid it when you only had three men driving a herd of forty or so head.

The canyon they were following spilled into a steep-sided valley that led in turn onto a wide, sweeping stretch of pastureland. Here Longarm turned loose the horses they had borrowed and the second herd they had acquired. After a few shouts from them, the herd ambled on toward the fresh pasture, drawn by the scent of water and the need for fresh graze. Longarm figured it would be sunset before any Circle D riders overtook them.

Meanwhile, it would look to Ellison as if he were being raided by two separate bands of rustlers. Before long his riders would be bringing him news of the newly branded cattle, and Denton would have some hard explaining to do.

As the herd disappeared finally behind the cloud of dust it raised, Longarm turned to Tomlinson and Hunnicut. "I'm going to head for the Circle D," he told them. "I want to watch what happens next. Maybe this crazy deception will set Ellison against Denton, and maybe it won't. Anyway, you two have done all you can. Get back to town and keep your eyes open."

"Suits me," Tomlinson said. "I got a stage line to run. Jane must be run ragged by now."

"You sure you don't want me to stay out here with you," Hunnicut asked Longarm.

"Thanks, Hunnicut. I won't need you. Ride in with

Tommy and keep your eyes open and your ass down. When this thing blows, we'll need you."

Without further comment, Hunnicut and Tomlinson turned their horses and moved off and were soon heading east over the grassland. Longarm watched until they were out of sight, then headed for Ellison's ranch.

As the sun moved, Hook inched himself still farther out onto the rock he had been lying on for the past three hours. To anyone watching from a distance, he bore an uncanny resemblance to a large lizard sunning itself.

Hook's lidded eyes were half-shut. It wasn't the sun, it was boredom. Ordinarily, he did not mind waiting—it came with the territory—but waiting for Frank Ellison to emerge from his ranch house was beginning to pall. The man as a cripple, and it was almost impossible to catch him in the open without someone hovering close by.

Denton had promised Hook a simple, uncomplicated assignment—to assassinate Frank Ellison. But when Hook had arrived in Sand Hills, Denton had been unwilling to go through with it. Ellison, it seemed, was a very powerful man in this territory. So Denton had given Hook other, more troublesome chores. Like stopping that stage and shooting up the driver. But now Denton was in some kind of crazy trouble with Ellison, something about him changing to his own wheel brand the brands on some Circle D cattle. It wasn't his doing, he told Hook, but it was close enough to the truth to make it impossible to explain. So last night Denton told Hook to take out Ellison before his partner caused him more trouble than he could handle.

As far as Hook was concerned, it was about time.

Too many people were getting good, long looks at him, and that could be bad for his business. But now, his money belt pleasantly heavy with his two-thousand-dollar fee, Hook found himself contemplating with pleasure his return to his horse ranch in Wyoming. He wanted to see again those green, timbered slopes and was sorry he had ever left them.

Hook's reptilian eyes came alert suddenly as he peered into the distance. A buggy was moving out of the Circle D compound. Hook waited, his eyes focusing on the figure driving the single trotter. When he saw the driver turn the buggy onto the trace and head for Sand Hills, he smiled. His patience had been rewarded. He was sure of it. He lifted a pair of binoculars to his eyes. Sure enough. The driver of the buggy was the crippled old bird himself, Frank Ellison.

Five minutes later, with Ellison's buggy approaching the entrance to the canyon just below him, Hook slipped back off the rock, heading for a spot he had already selected farther down the slope, closer to the canyon floor.

His long wait was over. He could already smell Wyoming's pine-scented slopes.

Longarm had spent three days camped on a pine ridge above Ellison's ranch, watching the frantic coming and going his ruse had initiated. He'd seen two lone riders gallop in the first day, and not long after that a single rider. After each alarm, bunches of Ellison's men had ridden out, Ellison's foreman leading the largest contingent. Longarm had glimpsed Ellison only twice in all that time, on each occasion leaning heavily on his crutches. The cattleman had visited the horse barn for a while, then gone back inside, the Zuni woman close by his side throughout.

That same afternoon two punchers hazed a weary steer into the compound, and Frank Ellison hobbled out to view personally Tomlinson's artistry with a running iron. After that, Longarm had expected to see a rider heading into Sand Hills to summon Bull Denton for an accounting. Instead, Ellison was soon being helped into his buggy by the Zuni woman, and a moment later, cracking his whip over the horse's back, Frank Ellison set out for Sand Hills himself.

Keeping in the timber above the trace, Longarm followed Ellison. If he was going into Sand Hills, Longarm decided it would be a good idea if he went along too. It wouldn't do any harm to keep an eye on Ellison. Denton was dangerously unpredictable, and if Ellison was going in to have it out with him, there might be trouble—trouble a man on crutches might not be able to handle.

Through the trees on the slope below him, Longarm saw Ellison approaching a canyon. Its slopes were crumbling, and since this would mean hard going for his mount, Longarm decided he would leave this slope and take the trace through the canyon, once Ellison was out of sight on the other side.

Breaking out of the timber, Longarm set his horse down the grassy slope. The sun was behind him, and lifting his gaze momentarily to the canyon wall ahead, he caught movement on a projecting leaf of rock. A second later he saw a man, a thin blade of a man, moving down the canyon wall, the sun glinting off the rifle he was carrying.

James B. Hook.

As Hook moved down the side of the canyon, displaced shale slipped out from underfoot. Apparently, he was making for a grassy ridge overlooking the trace, angling for a spot closer to the canyon floor, and in that instant Longarm knew why Denton had brought in Hook. It was to assassinate Frank Ellison, and Longarm's ruse had only served to accelerate matters.

Longarm pulled his rifle from its boot, then kicked his mount to a full gallop. Levering rapidly, his reins tied around his saddle horn, he sent a rapid fire up at the canyon wall, hoping not only to distract Hook, but to warn Ellison. Hearing Longarm's rifle fire, Ellison pulled his buggy to a halt and looked back at Longarm charging now across the flat as he approached the canyon.

Ellison apparently thought Longarm was firing at him and quickly reached down to pull his rifle off the floor of his buggy. Ignoring this, Longarm continued to pour fire at the canyon wall, spraying the area where he had last glimpsed Hook. And then he was inside the canyon, and no longer able to fire effectively at the spot where he had last glimpsed Hook.

"Pull your buggy around!" Longarm cried, galloping toward Ellison. "Make for cover! Hook's up there with a rifle."

Recognizing Longarm, Ellison brought up his rifle and peered up at the canyon wall.

At that moment, from high above came the sharp crack of Hook's rifle. The searing whiplash of a bullet jolted Longarm as it grazed his inner thigh and plunged through the neck of his horse, shattering his spine. As the horse collapsed under him, Longarm kicked loose of the stirrups and flung himself to the right. He landed crouching on a patch of sand and gravel, his rifle still in his hands, and darted for the canyon wall and the protection it afforded, two more rounds exploding the ground behind him. And then he was close in under the canyon wall, safe from fire coming from above.

But Ellison was not so lucky.

The owner of the Circle D was reaching for his crutch and trying to get out of the buggy and keep his rifle all at the same time. Then, in a fury of frustration, he threw the rifle out ahead of him, swung himself out of the buggy, and dragging the crutch around, started hobbling toward the rifle and the safety of the canyon wall.

Hook's first bullet caught Ellison in the side. He dropped his crutch and crumpled to the canyon floor. But he was game. He began to crawl toward the rifle and was within a few yards of it, his arm fully extended as he reached out, when two more carefully placed bullets smashed into his back, raising two small puffs of dust.

Ellison made no outcry. He put his head down and lay perfectly still, his body seeming to settle into the canyon floor. The echoes of Hook's last shot faded and the canyon became as silent as a tomb.

Chapter 9

Longarm looked about him at the crumbling canyon wall and saw a narrow trail that might lead up to the crest while giving him some protection from Hook's fire from above. Winchester in hand, he scrambled swiftly up the trail, grabbing hold of bushes and the exposed roots of gnarled pines as he hauled himself up the steep slope. At times he had to feel his way across nearly perpendicular rock faces, and once almost lost his rifle as a loose fragment of rock pulled out and went clattering noisily down the wall.

Until this happened he had made very little sound. Cursing silently, he froze flat against the wall of rock, aware that Hook could not have failed to hear the small avalanche he had initiated. Longarm waited for Hook to open up on him. But no shots came. Evidently Longarm was still not visible to him.

Longarm resumed his climb, and once past the rock he found the slope less sheer, allowing him to make better time as he pulled and clawed himself swiftly higher. Abruptly he heard the clash of metal on metal as Hook, high above him on the canyon's rim, cranked a fresh cartridge into his firing chamber. Longarm dove under an earthen ledge as Hook's rifle cracked. A portion of the slope only inches behind Longarm's boot disintegrated. A second round drove into the earthen brow over Longarm's head, showering him with sand and gravel. As the sand sifted off his hat brim, he ducked in still closer to the canyon's damp wall and waited.

But that was all. There were no more shots. Hook was no fool. No sense in firing at what he couldn't see.

Craning his head around, he peered up at a massive, wrinkled sheet of caprock directly above him that extended clear to the crest of the canyon wall at close to a forty-five degree angle. Deep, weathered cracks lined its ancient face. Once on that rock, if Longarm could keep moving fast enough and use those deep cracks for protection, he might be able to race the last thirty or so yards to the crest and catch Hook off guard.

Only first he had to get from where he was to the rock face. He leaned his head back against the wall behind him and gave it some thought. After a while he looked back the way he had come and studied the clump of scrub pine on the crest from behind which Hook's shots had come. The pines were well off to the right, but well within range of his rifle.

Swiftly, he considered his options and made his decision.

He stepped boldly out of cover, and levering swiftly

began pouring a fierce fusilade into the pines. He saw branches sheared, pine needles falling, and lower down, the tops of bunchgrass being cut away. He kept up the withering fire until he was close to empty, then abruptly hauled down his rifle and vaulted up the steep slope.

In a moment he was on the rock face, crouched low, moving swiftly along a massive crack that appeared to reach clear to the top. He followed it almost at a run. Ten yards from the top, it ran out. The rest of the way he would have to make in full view. His only hope was that Hook—his head down as a result of Longarm's fire—had not seen him dart onto the caprock. Clambering out onto the smooth rock, Longarm raced up the steep rock for the canyon's rim.

And then there was no more rock under his feet. Longarm vaulted onto the canyon rim and saw Hook crouching less than twenty yards farther down. He had heard Longarm's boots slapping the caprock as he raced up its steep incline. He flung his rifle up to his shoulder. Longarm threw himself to one side as Hook fired, hit the ground, rolled over, and came up behind a massive pile of bounders, unscathed. Hook's second round ricocheted off a boulder.

Longarm did not stay put behind the boulders. He circled around the boulders, intending to catch Hook with his back to the canyon rim. But Hook saw what he was about and raced off down the rim to escape Longarm's encirclement. Longarm took after the sound of his pounding feet. Just after he caught a glimpse of Hook, the man vanished completely, as if he had dropped into a hole.

A moment later, Longarm found himself looking down into a steep ravine, the trail leading into it winding out of sight behind scrub pine and wild grapevines. Longarm glimpsed Hook's hat moving out of sight and plunged down after him, but he had not gone more than halfway before he heard the echoing clatter of hooves and held up.

Hook had reached his horse.

Through a break in the pines, Longarm could see the floor of the gorge. Abandoning the trail, he raced out onto a ledge and gained a wider view of the ravine floor. Hook flashed into view, lashing his mount. Longarm flung up his rifle, tracked Hook, and squeezed off a shot. Hook slumped forward, but remained in the saddle. Horse and rider vanished.

Slowly, Longarm lowered his rifle.

He had winged Hook. He was sure of that. For now, that would have to do. Longarm had an unpleasant chore to take care of, and he wasn't looking forward to it. He turned and made his way back out of the gorge.

With all that gunfire, the horse had not bolted. The buggy waited in the rutted trace still, the horse calmly cropping the grass at its feet. Longarm removed his saddle and the rest of his gear from the dead horse and lugged them over to the buggy, shoving them under the front seat. Then he went for Frank Ellison. The rancher's dead weight made it difficult, but Longarm managed to throw Ellison over his shoulder and let him down on the buggy floor behind the front seat. Picking up Ellison's rifle, he placed that down on the buggy floor beside Ellison's corpse.

The flesh wound in the inside of Longarm's thigh was scabbing over, but it still smarted, and coagulated blood had already formed a hard shield on the inside of his thigh. He had been lucky to escape serious injury from Hook's fire and knew it.

He stepped up onto the buggy's seat, turned the horse, and started back to the ranch house. He was halfway there when he saw the Zuni woman driving a spring wagon out to meet him, a Circle D rider up on the seat beside her. She was not sparing the two horses. The gunfire must have carried to the ranch, and the woman, worried, was hurrying to investigate. Longarm pulled up and got down to wait for them to reach him.

The man with her handed her down with great respect, and then turned with some belligerence to face Longarm; the Zuni woman was frowning anxiously as she shaded her eyes and looked up at him. Neither she nor the ranch hand had looked beyond him to what lay behind the buggy's front seat.

"What the hell are you doing with this buggy?" the cowpuncher demanded.

"Where's Frank?" the woman asked in beautifully modulated English. It was the first time he had heard her utter a sound.

"Look behind the seat," Longarm told them. He did not know how else to break it to them.

At these words, the Zuni woman darted past Longarm to the buggy. One look at the crumpled body and she stopped in her tracks, gasping audibly; then she threw herself on the man's dead body, crying out. In a moment, she had Ellison's white-maned head in her lap as she rocked unconsolably, keening out her lament.

The cowpuncher turned on Longarm. He didn't know whether to cry out himself or lunge at Longarm. "Dammit, mister! What've you done?"

Longarm held up his hand. "You're not thinking very

clear, mister. I am not responsible for Frank Ellison's death."

"How the hell do I know that?"

"Now what in the hell makes you think I'd be fool enough to bring back in his own buggy the corpse of the man I just murdered?"

"Well, goddamn it, if you didn't do it, who did?"

"One of Bull Denton's hired guns. A man called Hook."

"You saw him do it?"

"You mean did I stand around watching? No. I tried to warn Ellison, but all I got for my pains was my horse shot out from under me and this thigh wound."

The puncher saw the dried blood behind the rip in Longarm's pants, then scratched his head in perplexity. "Dammit, mister, this don't make no sense. I just got up and found everyone lit out. I don't know what the hell's going on. But mister, Denton is Ellison's partner. Why in hell would he want to kill him?"

"First things first," Longarm told him wearily, turning to gaze at the grieving woman. "We've got to get this woman and your dead boss back to the ranch house and send into Sand Hills for the undertaker. Then I want to speak to your foreman. As soon as he gets back, that is."

"Sanchez?"

"That's the man. I don't think he'll find this so hard to believe."

Hook lashed his horse on through the night. In the bright moonlight, the trace was easily visible, stretching ahead of him as far as the horizon. He knew he might kill his mount at the pace he was setting, but he had no choice. The bullet Longarm had sent into him had lodged in the muscle just back of his left shoulder, and with every jolting pound of his horse's hooves, the slug seemed to burrow in deeper, like a small, voracious animal.

This was the first time he had ever been wounded, and it astonished him as much as it angered him. He could feel the blood oozing steadily down his back, gathering heavily at his belt. It was because he was losing so much blood that he was returning to Sand Hills instead of riding out as he had planned. He needed a doctor—and the help that Denton could provide in killing that meddling son of a bitch who had done this to him. He smiled grimly at the thought. Now that he had a personal stake in a killing, he found it gave him more of a kick.

This one he'd do for nothing, just personal satisfaction.

He continued on through the darkness at a hard, steady gallop, gritting his teeth as the bullet continued to work its way still deeper into his shoulder.

Longarm's description of the shooting finished, Pablo Sanchez shook his head, got up from his chair, and began to pace. They were in Ellison's big cool living room, where the cattleman had entertained Longarm and Jane not so long ago.

It was late, near midnight, and the foreman had not had much of a chance to pull himself together after viewing Frank Ellison's body. He had already sent one of his men into Sand Hills for a priest to conduct the burial services, but he was still profoundly shocked by Ellison's death. The Zuni woman was in her room, her

135

two sons with her, offering her what comfort they could.

Pablo stopped his pacing and turned to face Longarm.

"This man, Hook. You say you wounded him?"

"I'm pretty sure of it."

"I hope so, *señor* Drake. I hope so. But I want even more to get this Bull Denton. As you say, he is the man behind all this."

"You don't find that hard to believe, then."

"No, *señor,* I do not. Denton's men, they use running iron on Circle D cattle. But this Denton, he is a greedy man. Impatient. So he bring in this man Hook to kill Frank.

"That's how it looks, all right."

"Now what you think we do about thees?"

"Get your men together and we'll ride into Sand Hills."

"For what purpose, *señor?*"

"I want you or one of your men to take the stage to Socorro and send a telegram to the territorial governor in Santa Fe. It's about time the county sheriff made a visit, no matter how many miles away his office is."

"There will not be so many to ride in with us, I think."

"How come?"

"Without Frank, thees men say they are at the mercy of Denton and his hired gunslicks. It is not easy for some men to be loyal to a dead man."

"What about you?"

"I will ride in with you and take the stage to Socorro. But first, maybe you tell me one thing?"

"What is it, Pablo?"

"Why are you in this? What did Bull Denton do to you?"

"It's not him I want as much as Hook."

Pablo's black eyes lit. "He is a killer, that one. I see him in town. Like a shadow out of hell. He kill someone you know?"

"Tried to. The owner of the stage line. Tomlinson."

Sanchez nodded emphatically. "Tomorrow. After we bury *señor* Ellison, we ride into Sand Hills."

"That suits me."

Dawn had not yet lightened the eastern sky when Hook clattered into town. Dismounting, he led his horse down the alley in back of the barbershop, leaving the lathered animal in the small barn provided by the barber. Too weak to unsaddle the horse, Hook slapped it into its stall, left it, and clambered unsteadily up the back stairs to his room. Since he had not told the barber he was leaving Sand Hills for good when he rode out four days earlier, no explanation was needed as he closed the door behind him, then lurched over to the bed and collapsed facedown onto it, passing out almost at once.

He awoke with the sun high, the ache in his shoulder intolerable. He was feverish and as weak as a cat. He unbuckled his money belt, then pushed himself off the bed and put the belt in the bureau's top drawer. Then he went to the door and stepped out onto the wooden landing. One glance down the steep staircase and he decided against trying to negotiate it. He went back inside for his old rifle, returned, and began slamming the barrel against the side of the building just below the landing. He kept it up doggedly until the barber Enrico appeared

137

in his shop's back door. His apron still on, a pair of scissors in his hand, his shiny black hair slicked down.

"What you want, Mr. Hook?"

"Send the doc up here—and get Bull Denton."

The man frowned. "You want I should go—?"

"Just *do* it!" Hook told him and ducked back into his room, slamming the door behind him.

Sitting down on the edge of his bed, he carefully took off his frock coat, then the vest and shirt, each movement sending rocking spasms of pain through his shoulders and midriff. This done, he kicked off his boots and lay back on the cot, unmindful of the growing stain of fresh blood spreading over the bedclothes from under his shoulder.

He lost track of time, but it seemed he had just lain his head back when there came an urgent knock on his door. He called out for the knocker to enter, and the doc strode in, carrying his black bag. Behind him came Denton, the Kid on his heels.

Without sitting up, Hook said, "I took a slug in my shoulder, Doc. Get the son of a bitch out before I bleed to death."

Saying nothing, the doc opened his bag, set it down on a dresser beside the cot, then turned Hook over onto his stomach to examine the wound. He was still saying nothing when, after a good two minutes of probing, he caught the bullet in his forceps and withdrew it.

By that time the pain had caused Hook to pass out.

As soon as the doctor proceeded to wash the wound out with a solution of carbolic and salt, however, the pain dragged Hook, moaning fearfully, back to full consciousness.

Watching the doctor finish bandaging Hook's

shoulder, Denton and the Kid both detected a grim smile on the doc's face as he noted his patient's low but urgent outcries. A moment before, when the doc had probed for the bullet, he had not been at all gentle, and he had sure as hell taken his time. The doc was not on their side, they realized. But there was nothing they could do about it. The doc was one man they all needed.

As the doc started from the room, Denton stepped forward and handed him a bill. The doc crumpled it, dropped it to the floor, and left.

"The son of a bitch," Hook said, sitting up painfully. "He enjoyed making me cry uncle."

"Yeah," said the Kid. "But he got the slug out."

"What in hell happened?" Denton asked. "Did you get Ellison?"

"I got him. You don't have to worry about that."

"You mean he shot you up? There was a shoot-out?"

"No. It was that goddamn meddler, the one says he wants to buy into the stage line."

"Drake?"

"That's the one."

"What the hell was he doing out there?"

"How the hell should I know."

"Maybe you better explain, give me a better picture."

"Hell, Denton. All I know is I've got Ellison all lined up in my sights and this guy Drake comes riding out of nowhere, shooting up at me and yelling a warning to Ellison."

"So you killed them both?"

"No. I caught Drake's horse and he went diving for cover. But after I sent three bullets into Ellison, Drake came up the wall after me, and I lit out. That man is spooky."

"How'd you get the bullet?"

"While I was riding off. He's some shot, damn his hide."

"And that means you got a witness to the killing."

"That's right."

"A witness who's still alive and kicking. Christ, Hook, that means we'll have to take care of him when he gets back in here."

Hook nodded grimly. "I was thinkin' you might say that."

The Kid grinned at Hook. "And it won't cost you a thing," he said, rubbing the side of his face where Jud Drake had kicked him.

Chapter 10

The day after the burial of Frank Ellison, Longarm and Pablo Sanchez arrived in Sand Hills. They had set out early that morning and arrived at the express office after dark. The town was well into its nightly bacchanal, with Denton's armed hoodlums keeping order with a surprisingly loose rein. To Longarm, clopping down the main street and viewing the wild revelry on all sides, it seemed the town was enjoying a hectic, almost delirious sense of abandon.

Longarm had no doubt why this was. Bull Denton no longer had Frank Ellison to restrain him. With his partner's death, Denton was now the sole owner of the partnership's lands and enterprises. And it was as if the townsmen and their nightly celebrants sensed his jubilation and were joining him in it.

Pulling up in front of the darkened express office, the

two men dismounted. Dropping their reins over the hitch rail, they mounted the porch steps. Longarm knocked loudly on the express door, knocked again, then peered through the windows into the unlighted gloom. For a moment he had the alarming fear that Denton, in a sudden fit of hubris, might have decided to wait no longer and simply take over the line. Who or what, after all, was left to stop him?

Longarm was about to knock again when the inner door opened and Tomlinson, a shotgun under one arm, entered the office, crossed quickly to the door, and flung it open.

"Well, Drake!" he cried, obviously relieved. "We was wonderin' what had happened to you. Come in! Come in!"

Longarm introduced Sanchez to Tomlinson, then followed the old man through the office and up to their apartment. Jane was at the stove when Longarm tramped in. She put down the coffeepot she was filling and rushed into his arms, making no effort to hide her pleasure at his arrival. Jimmy Hunnicut was sitting at the table in front of a huge platter of doughnuts. He got to his feet and shook hands with Sanchez as Longarm introduced the man to him and Jane.

At first everyone tried to talk at once, but held up quickly at the futility of it. Longarm then sat down at the table, accepted a cup of coffee from Jane, and proceeded to describe the assassination of Frank Ellison. After that he told them of Pablo Sanchez's upcoming mission to Socorro, in order to telegraph Santa Fe, so they could get some much-needed law into this part of the county.

When he finished, a nervous and very unhappy Tomlinson cleared his throat. "Sorry, Drake," he said rue-fully, "but there won't be no stage out of here for some time."

"Why not?"

"That deal you worked out with Denton is gone by the board," Tomlinson replied. "Hook's in town and I guess he told Denton what you did out there. He knows sure as hell you ain't throwin' in with him. So there's no more dealing. Denton says not a stagecoach of ours can leave this express office until we sign the line over to him."

"And of course we refused," Jane snapped.

"And that's why you were lugging that shotgun when you came down to let us in."

"It is. And I've warned Denton that if any of his monkeys come messing around this office, they'll get a load of double-aught buckshot up their asses—excuse me, Jane."

"That's perfectly all right, Dad."

Longarm looked at Pablo. "You'll just have to make the trip to Socorro on horseback, then."

Pablo nodded. "I will leave in the morning. Re-member, you say you will write telegram for me."

"I'll write it out tonight."

"He's goin' to have trouble getting out of town," said Jane, looking with some concern at Pablo.

"Now what?" Longarm asked.

"Two Circle D riders rode in last night. They went straight to the Silverado and spilled their guts about Frank's death, and the fact that Pablo was going to tele-graph the sheriff. Denton then let it be known that no one was going to ride out of here to telegraph anybody."

"If you do manage to get out of town, Pablo, he's

143

probably got men along the trail waiting for you," said Hunnicut.

"And in Socorro," added Tomlinson.

"I should not have mention it," Pablo said ruefully. "But I only tell one of my men."

"That kind of news gets around fast," Longarm remarked.

"So what do we do?" Tomlinson asked nervously.

"We're trapped," said Hunnicut. "Andy and the boys have already left. Slade visited them and the two jehus, and we ain't seen any of them since."

"So now you're holed up here, waiting."

Jane nodded gloomily.

"You can't let Denton call the shots like this," Longarm told them. "If you stay here, like rats in a trap, there's nothing you can do—except wait for Denton and his hired guns to march in here and clean you out." Longarm glanced at Jane. "What about Hook? You say he's back here?"

"Yes," Jane said. "You were right. You did wing him. In the shoulder. Doc says he lost a lot of blood."

"But he's up and around now," Hunnicut told Longarm. "I went into the Silverado this evening without my badge on to look around. I kept my ass down and didn't ask any questions. But I saw Hook. He looked the same. Black hat, coat, and britches, a cigar in his mouth, and his rifle leaning against the wall."

"He's done what Denton brought him in for," Longarm noted, "and he should be on his way. But it looks like he's decided he has other business to take care of first."

"That's right," said Jane. "You."

Longarm thought things over for a moment, all eyes

144

on him, waiting. "We don't have the firepower to cut them all down at once. We'll just have to split up and take out Denton and his cutthroats one at a time, before they have enough sense to march on us together."

"You have a plan?" Tomlinson asked.

Longarm nodded. "If you can call it that. We'll go after the head of this serpent first. I'll take out Hook. Jimmy, you take out the Kid. Tommy, you see if you can neutralize Slade, assuming he's up and about now."

"He is," snapped Tomlinson. "He looks like you dragged him through a meat grinder, but he's movin' around and meaner than a rattler."

Longarm looked at Pablo. "You said you wanted to get the man who sent Hook after Frank."

Pablo nodded decisively.

"Do you know this town well, and the Silverado?"

"I have been here many times with my men. Often I drink in the Silverado."

"And you know how to get up to Denton's office?"

Pablo's dark face smiled, the black eyes glinting. "Yes, I know that."

Jane looked from one face to another in pure astonishment. "My God, Jud! You mean you expect us to walk around assassinating people?"

"Not you," Longarm replied. "And it sure as hell won't be as simple as that."

"Hey, now, wait a minute. You can't leave me out of this."

Longarm smiled at her sudden change of tone. "All right, then. We won't."

"So how we going to do it?" Hunnicut asked nervously.

"We'll need a diversion."

"What kind?"

"A good fire should do nicely."

"What are we going to burn? The Silverado?"

"No. It's in too close to the buildings alongside it. Innocent people might get hurt."

"What then?" asked Jane.

"The stage line's horse barn!"

Jane gasped.

Her father said, "Hey, now! Wait just a minute."

"There'll be no horses inside when we set it off, and everything of value we'll haul out beforehand. Look at it this way, what we'll really be doing is torching Denton's latest acquisition."

"Which means," admitted Tomlinson grudgingly, "that he and his men will come running."

"That's the idea." Longarm leaned back in his chair and looked around at the others. "We're agreed then?"

"We're agreed," said Jane gloomily. "I just hope when all this is over we'll have enough money to put up another barn."

"Another barn and a larger barn. That's a promise."

That ended the preliminaries. Jane made more coffee and they got down to particulars.

It was two in the morning. The gambling halls and saloons and parlor houses were emptying out. The miners were crowding onto high-sided ore wagons for the long pounding ride back to the silver mine, punchers were pouring themselves onto their horses and riding out of town, and homesteaders were going home to face the music.

Meanwhile, Longarm and the others had been working furiously since Longarm outlined his plan. They transferred most of the hay, feed, pitchforks, and other implements to the second big corral, the one behind the warehouse. The other corral was too close to the horse barn and would not be as safe for the horses.

That completed, Jane and Hunnicut crouched down behind a horse trough. Jane had a carbine and Hunnicut a double-barreled shotgun. Leaving them to watch the horses, Tomlinson and Longarm climbed to the barn's loft, lit the lanterns they were carrying, then sent them flying against the rafters. As the lamps shattered, there was a muffled *whump* and flames exploded down onto the hay and leaped up one wall.

The two men hurried back to the corral, saw to it that Jane and Hunnicut had the horses under control, then moved into the alley and crouched down to wait.

Pablo Sanchez was sitting at a small table in the corner of the Silverado. The games of chance were quiet, the poker tables empty, and the bar girls had left with whomever they had managed to snare at the last moment. A few patrons were still hunched up to the bar. The barkeep was reminding them it was closing time when a townsman burst through the batwings.

"Fire!" he cried. "Fire!"

"Where?"

"At the stagecoach stables!"

The patrons downed what was left in their glasses and stormed out of the saloon to watch, the barkeep following, and soon the night was filled with the cry to form up a bucket brigade. Stampeding feet thundered past the saloon as up and down the street cries filled the night. The tumult faded rapidly, and then it was reasonably quiet just outside the saloon.

Sanchez finished his drink and waited.

Upstairs in his office, Denton heard the outcry, followed by the thunder of boots as the patrons stampeded from the saloon. He went to his window and looking out saw the glow lighting the sky farther down the street.

He flung up his window and yelled down to someone racing up the alley, "Where's the fire!"

"The express office!"

Denton slammed down the window, thinking at once of the warehouse, the barn, and all those horses, and was astounded that Tomlinson and his daughter would take such a drastic step just to prevent him from taking over the line. For there was no doubt in his mind that this was indeed what they were doing.

His astonishment gave way to rage. Snatching up his gun belt, he buckled it on and charged out of his office, yelling, "Kid!"

The Kid had been asleep on the sofa in the living room, but he was on his feet, his hat on his head, and fully awake by the time Denton poked his head into the room.

"Where's Slade?"

"Downstairs somewhere."

"Get him. We're going to make them two pay for this!"

"Pay for what? Who?"

"Tomlinson and his daughter. They just set fire to our new stage line!"

"I'll get Slade!" the Kid cried, ducking down the hallway ahead of Denton.

Denton followed out onto the balcony after him and saw the Kid charging down the stairs, vanishing through the batwings an instant later. Denton himself was about to descend the stairs when he saw Sanchez sitting at a corner table in the now-empty saloon. The Circle D foreman looked up as Denton paused on the landing and smiled, his greaser's mustache making him look almost satanic.

And just about as deadly. Denton was no fast-draw, quick-shooting marvel. He couldn't hit a fence post at twenty paces, and knew it—which was why he hired others to do his shooting for him.

He decided his best bet was to stall and hope someone would come in to bail him out. "What do you want?" Denton called down.

"Don't you know, *señor?*"

He was always a polite bastard, Denton recalled nervously, his thoughts charging about wildly as he tried to figure a way to slow this son of a bitch down. He had no idea how good Sanchez was with a gun, but he had to be better than he was.

"You think I had something to do with Frank's death. Is that it?"

Sanchez got to his feet and strode casually across the floor toward the stairs. "You say you did not send thees man Hook to kill Frank?"

"I swear. I had nothing to do with it!"

"Do you swear on the sacred memory of your mother?"

"Sure! Sure, I do!"

"You never had a mother! You were born of a snake and suckled by a pig!"

As he spoke he drew his revolver, a huge son of a bitch that looked like an ancient Walker Colt. At that instant one of Denton's armed guards pushed through the batwings, his rifle at the ready. He took one look at Sanchez and cried, "Hey, you over there!"

Sanchez spun, the gun jumping in his hand as he pumped two rounds into the guard's chest. The startled gunman dropped his rifle and stumbled back out through the batwings. Without pause Sanchez flung himself about and fired up at Denton. But Denton was already ducking back from the stairwell, and the bullet glanced off a balustrade.

"Come on up here, Sanchez," Denton taunted, his mouth suddenly dry. "I'm waiting for you."

Denton was holding his weapon as steadily as he could manage, but panic was turning his knees to water and making his hands tremble. The Colt Sanchez was using had sounded like a cannon, and the sight of that guard flipping back out through the batwings had sent a shiver of pure terror down Denton's back.

Turning, he bolted into his apartment, raced down the hallway and into his living room. Slamming the door behind him, he flung a heavy leather armchair against the door, then ducked down behind the sofa, panting with terror.

Sanchez paused just below the landing. For all his bluster and treachery, this Denton acted now like a frightened rabbit. But Sanchez was no fool. A coward was unpredictable and could be very dangerous. Carefully, he peered over the lip of the landing at the balcony beyond. About twenty feet farther down, the door leading to Denton's apartment was wide open, and Sanchez expected Denton to be just inside, waiting to blast him. If so, it was a chance he had to take.

He swept up the stairs onto the balcony and flattened himself against the wall. But there was no fusilade from the open door. Denton must have ducked farther into his apartment. Sanchez was about to charge on down the balcony and through the door when from below came the tramp of heavy boots. Leaning over the bannister, he saw two of Denton's henchmen, carbines in hand, charging across the floor toward the staircase. Before they thought to look up, Sanchez sent one round through the head of the one in front, and as the other slewed to a frantic stop and flung up his carbine, Sanchez calmly shot him in the chest, then the neck.

As both men slumped to the floor, Sanchez reloaded his Walker. When no more of Denton's men charged into the saloon—the fire had evidently drawn everyone too far down the street to hear the shots—he ducked swiftly into Denton's apartment and closed the door behind him. He did not want to be disturbed. He knew that Denton's office was down the end of the hallway, and flattened himself against the wall and peered down the unlit corridor. The open doorway leading into Denton's office was a black, rectangular hole.

When no shots erupted from that black rectangle, Sanchez moved down the hallway and came to a closed door. He had visited Denton many times with Frank Ellison and knew that this door led into the living room. Slowly, Sanchez turned the knob and then pushed, and felt the door come against something solid propped against it. It felt like a heavy, upholstered chair. He smiled, his white teeth gleaming in his swarthy face.

Denton was forted up in this room.

Even as he thought this, two detonations shattered the silence in the room beyond the door. Inches from his head two splintered holes appeared in the door, and the wall behind him exploded as shards of plaster showered down. He ducked swiftly as another blast sounded in the room, but this round expended itself into the barrier propped against the door.

Sanchez was pleased. He could push open the door and use the chair as a shield. Still keeping down, he rested his shoulder against the door and began to push, and felt the chair on the other side moving into the room as it slowly, steadily gave way before Sanchez's steady pressure.

Behind the sofa Denton saw the door beginning to open. He swallowed, or tried to, then looked for a way out of the corner he had been driven into, and saw the door leading to his bedroom. In the bedroom was another door leading to his office, and from his office he would have an unobstructed view into the hallway.

He pushed out from behind the sofa, kicked off his shoes, and slipped swiftly into the bedroom, and from there into his office. He was careful to make not a sound as he stepped across it to the doorway opening out onto the long hallway.

There was no light in the hallway, but by this time his sight was almost preternaturally keen, enabling him to see Sanchez, partially upright, getting ready to push the living room door all the way open. Stepping into the doorway, Denton raised his revolver, aimed carefully, and fired. The gun bucked wildly into the air, the detonation filling the narrow hallway and almost deafening him. When the smoke cleared, Denton saw with horror that he had missed Sanchez and that Sanchez was on his feet, driving swiftly toward him. The weight of his revolver brought it down again, the barrel pointed straight at the oncoming foreman, and again, desperately, Denton pulled the trigger.

The first bullet fired by Denton had not missed. The round had punched into Sanchez's left side and slammed him sideways against the doorjamb.

Turning about, he lurched to his feet and charged down the hallway at Denton, dimly aware that his left leg was not responding as it should. Another blast thundered in the narrow hallway. Sanchez felt a second punch, this one in his gut. Both legs shot out from under him and he went down with the suddenness of a horse stepping into a gopher hole. The point of his jaw struck the carpetless floor, stunning him. Blinking away the darkness that threatened to engulf him, he hauled his revolver around and fired up at Denton—still looming in the doorway—thumb-cocked and fired again. Denton buckled and vanished into the office. Sanchez heard the man slam against a solid piece of furniture, then the clatter of his gun as it struck the floor.

Sanchez dragged himself the rest of the way down the hallway and into the office, and saw Denton propped up crookedly on the arm of an easy chair, his back leaning against the wall. Crawling very slowly over the floor, he got close enough to reach up and grab Denton's ankle, and began tugging on him in an effort to pull him down beside him on the floor.

His exertions were causing slick coils of his intestines to spill out through the hole in his gut, but he ignored this and continued to tug on Denton's ankle, keeping at it even though he experienced periodic blackouts, until at last Denton slipped off the arm of the chair and slammed to the floor, faceup, one arm draped over Sanchez's ankle. Pulling himself around, Sanchez poked the barrel of his revolver into Denton's open mouth. Ignoring the man's muffled gasp as he revived and reached up to push away the revolver, Sanchez cocked and fired, then pulled himself closer and rested his head on Denton's chest and found there was no heartbeat.

"Gracias a Dios," he muttered, laid his head down on the floor, and died.

Chapter 11

Watching the flames leaping into the sky, aware of the heat searing his cheekbones, the Kid flung up his forearm to protect his eyes and backed up. Those trying to douse the fire with buckets of water began pulling away also. It wouldn't be long before the roof collapsed into the fire, causing flames and blazing cinders to shoot thirty or forty feet higher into the air.

The Kid had not found Slade, and where in the hell was Denton?

He looked back along the plaza. There was no one near the Silverado. He had thought Denton was right behind him.

"Kid!"

Turning, the Kid saw Slade hurrying toward him through the crowd. "Where's Denton?" Slade asked.

"Beats the shit out of me. I thought he left right behind me."

Slade was not concerned. "He's around here somewhere, then."

Pulling up beside the Kid, Slade shaded his eyes as he peered up at the vaulting flames, the blazing cinders lofting still higher into the night. The plaza fronting the barn had been turned into garish day.

"That roof is going any minute," the Kid said, taking a few steps back. "We better get back."

"Did anyone tell you yet?" Slade asked, keeping up with the Kid.

"Tell me what?"

"There were no horses in the barn. It was cleaned out. Tomlinson and that brat of his started this."

"That's the first thing Denton said."

"So where are the bastards?"

"My guess is they're hiding in back somewhere, maybe behind the warehouse, with the horses."

Slade looked at the Kid, his eyes gleaming in the blazing light. "I say we go get 'em. We'll never have a better chance. We can dump 'em in the barn afterward and everyone'll think they got caught in the fire."

The Kid liked it. Taking care of them two would put them in solid with Denton. "Let's go," he said, heading for the alley leading to the warehouse.

Tomlinson was alone with Hunnicut, crouched down behind the water trough. Earlier, Longarm had gone off to find Hook. It bothered him that Hook was nowhere to be seen, and he didn't like not knowing where he was. So Tomlinson had urged Longarm to leave him and go after Hook, while he went back to relieve Jane. He didn't like her out in the middle of this, even if she could handle that carbine better than most men.

She was up in the apartment now with orders to shoot anyone who might try to charge up those stairs into the apartment, not an unlikely idea considering what Denton's frame of mind would be about now, watching this barn he thought was his going up in flames. Jane saw the wisdom of this precaution and had left without protest. Relieved that Jane was out of danger, he was waiting now for developments with Hunnicut. So far, none of Denton's men had come looking for the horses, and that Tomlinson found surprising.

Abruptly, Hunnicut nudged him. "Here they come," he said.

"Where?"

Hunnicut pointed to a couple of crouching figures moving around the corner of the warehouse.

"It's Slade," said Tomlinson.

"And the Kid."

"Come into my parlor, said the spider to the fly." Tomlinson said, jacking a fresh cartridge into his Winchester's firing chamber.

"I just wish I had some nails in this shotgun," Hunnicut remarked.

"The buckshot will do it. Just keep it low, and remember you got two barrels."

"How we going to play this?"

"I don't want no shooting this close to the horses. They're already pretty skittish."

"So we move out."

Tomlinson indicated with a quick nod the outhouse farther down the alley. "I'm heading for over there. I should get a good shot as soon as they clear the yard."

"I'll head for that other corner of the warehouse, keep low, and get behind them."

"Watch out for them flames. It's pretty hot over there."

"Not as hot as I'm goin' to make it for them two."

"No more talk, Jimmy. Get moving."

Suiting action to words, Tomlinson slipped swiftly through the corral poles and headed for the outhouse.

The Kid pulled up, pointing. "There's the horses," he said. "All safe and sound."

"Denton'll be glad to know that."

"Forget Denton. Tomlinson should be around here, probably luggin' that shotgun of his."

"We better split up," Slade said. "You go over that way. I'll head for the back alley, get behind the corral."

"Neat," said the Kid. "Send me over where the flames'll put me in plain sight."

"And give you plenty of light to shoot by. Stop bellyachin' Kid, and get going."

The Kid moved off. Slade hesitated only an instant, then darted up to the corral, kept low, and peered through the poles. The horses, snorting and skittish at the smell of the fire, had bunched into a knot as far from the flames as they could get. He peered over at the horse trough. No one there, and that was strange. With no one to keep the horses from bolting, how could Tomlinson be sure they wouldn't break out or injure themselves trying?

With a shrug, he kept going.

•　•　•

Tomlinson saw Slade moving away from the corral toward him and couldn't believe it. Longarm had said this would be his man, and here he was walking right for him as big as life and twice as ugly. He held his breath, waited for Slade to get within fifteen yards, then stepped out from behind the outhouse.

And lost his nerve.

He should have fired—but couldn't. Instead, in a voice that betrayed his uncertainty, he cried out, "Hold it right there, Slade!"

Slade's only response was to dart to one side, throwing up his revolver and firing as he did so. The bullet slammed into Tomlinson, catching him high on the left shoulder and smashing him back against the outhouse with such force he thought the privy would move off its foundation. And then he was on the ground, firing his rifle at the darting shadow ahead of him, no longer afraid, only angry as he levered rapidly and kept on firing. He saw Slade go down suddenly, crying out in pain, then get up and race past the outhouse down the alley.

Tomlinson scrambled to his feet and took after him.

Hunnicut heard the shooting in the alley. So did the Kid. He moved out of the shadow of the warehouse and stepped closer to the corral. The Kid had not already drawn his guns, Hunnicut noticed. Apparently he was so sure of his quick draw he didn't feel the need to do so. Hunnicut let him get well clear of the shadows before he stepped into view himself.

"I'm over here, Kid."

The Kid froze, turned his head.

"Remember me?"

The Kid squinted. "That you, Hunnicut?"

Hunnicut realized then that with the flaming barn at his back, it was difficult for the Kid to make out his face. "Yeah, it's me, all right. Hunnicut. The town marshal."

The Kid chuckled as those attempting to fight the fire behind Hunnicut dropped their buckets and fled. A fire was bad enough without getting caught up in a gun duel.

"You heard me, Kid," Hunnicut said, his mouth suddenly very dry.

"I heard you might've thrown in with Tomlinson and his brat," the Kid told Hunnicut casually. "But I never saw you around much. Smart move that, keeping your ass down, I mean."

"It's not down now."

"You're still as yellow as a jar of mustard, Hunnicut. Why don't you drop that shotgun before it goes off and scares you."

"Why don't you stop talking—and draw?"

"Hell, this boy's mother didn't raise him up to be no fool. You got the drop on me, Marshal. I wouldn't have a chance. You know that."

Hunnicut was momentarily stymied. Confused. This wasn't the big shoot-out he had built himself up to expect. The Kid was cheating him. It was as if Hunnicut had stepped on a rattler, and the damned thing had refused to strike. Wouldn't even shake its rattles, in fact.

Hunnicut moistened his lips and felt his palms getting sweaty as they grasped the shotgun. "Then maybe you better drop them gun belts," he said.

"Now, why would I want to go and do a thing like that?"

"Because I said so, dammit! I'm still the marshal, don't forget."

The Kid turned cautiously until he was facing Hunnicut squarely. "Now, don't get your balls in an uproar, Marshal. No need to sweat it. Never could see the sense in standing up to a double-barreled shotgun."

The Kid's pale hands dropped to his belt buckle. Hunnicut took a step closer, hefting the shotgun nervously, and in that instant the Kid's hands left the belt buckle, and with a speed impossible to follow brought up two thundering weapons, their muzzles belching fire.

One bullet struck Hunnicut in the thigh.

Another hit him in the ribs, slamming him backward.

His head struck the ground behind him so sharply that ribbons of light danced before his eyes. He twisted about sideways and saw the Kid walking closer to him. Hunnicut had difficulty focusing his eyes. The Kid's face was glowing from the fire behind Hunnicut, and there was a grin on it. His two six-guns gleamed in the firelight as he trained them down at Hunnicut. From the look on the Kid's face, Hunnicut knew the Kid was going to finish him off, and he tried to push himself away and found his right hand was still holding the shotgun, his finger still on the triggers.

What the hell, he thought grimly. I got nothin' more to lose.

He flipped up the shotgun. The barrel was less than a foot from the Kid's midsection when he squeezed both triggers. The recoil tore the shotgun from his grasp, the buckshot slamming through the Kid with such force he was lifted off the ground. He hit the ground a moment later in two separate pieces.

The duel apparently over, the townsmen forgot the fire and ran over, forming a quick ring of curious faces staring down at him. Jane broke through the crowd and went down on her knees beside him.

"Jimmy! How bad are you hurt?"

"I caught two slugs. One in the leg, the other in my chest."

The doc materialized out of the night and gently pushed Jane aside as he proceeded to examine Hunnicut's wounds. After a swift but expert examination, he sat back on his heels.

"He'll live," the doc said, dropping his stethoscope into his black bag. "He's got a broken rib is all. The bullet ranged up into his chest, but it's not deep. I can get it out." He paid little attention to the thigh wound, got up, and waved two men closer. "Get him over to my office," he told them.

As Hunnicut was lifted off the ground, Jane leaned close to him. "What about Dad?" she cried anxiously. "Where is he?"

"Over there," Hunnicut managed. "Down that alley, last I saw."

Jane left him and pushed through the crowd. In a moment, the carbine in her hand, she was cutting past the outhouse, running full tilt down the alley.

Hook had gone out earlier and had spent an hour or so in the Silverado. But a weariness overtook him, and he returned to his room and was asleep almost instantly. The commotion from the fire was what awakened him, and he had pulled on his boots, snatched up his rifle, and gone out to see what was going on. Standing at the head of the alley that ran between the barbershop and the general store next to it, he watched the Silverado disgorge the few patrons remaining inside.

Hook had no intention of helping the townsmen douse the fire. It was the horse barn belonging to the stage line going up, and Hook had a pretty good idea why it had been set afire. And by whom. He saw the hand of that fellow Drake in this, too. If it was a ruse, Hook was not going to let himself be sucked in.

He saw the Kid race out of the Silverado and pound off toward the fire. Hook expected to see Denton follow right behind the Kid, but Denton did not show. Hook straightened. Where the hell was he? Had he already left? Hook hadn't seen Slade, either. A faint unease stirred in him, but he remained where he was. Three of Denton's guards had not caught the fever and remained in front of the Silverado. Loyal watchdogs.

The fire's glow increased dramatically as the flames bathed the underside of the heavy black pillar of smoke twisting into the night sky. The frantic townsmen running back and forth with their buckets reminded Hook of an ant colony rushing about after their hill had been stomped.

One of the three guards turned and went back into the Silverado. Hook was about to turn and go back up to his room when he heard two quick shots coming from inside the saloon. The guard who had just entered went reeling back out through the batwings. A third shot came from within. The other two guards crouched low, then moved cautiously toward the batwings. Hook lifted his rifle and levered a shell into the firing chamber and

163

watched as the two guards, hefting their carbines, debated whether or not to enter the saloon.

"Go on!" Hook muttered. "Get in there!"

Almost as if they had heard him, the two men straightened up and charged through the batwings. Hook heard them pounding across the saloon. Three quick shots followed and Hook thought he could hear the clatter of carbines striking the floor.

Then silence.

Down the street the fire became a conflagration. The activity more feverish. Hook looked back at the saloon and waited. But no more shots came from within. Cautiously, Hook crossed the street and mounted the saloon's porch. Stepping around the first guard who lay on his back beside the door, as dead as a fence post, he peered into the saloon over the tops of the batwings. The other two guards were on their backs, their blood mingling with the floor's sawdust.

Drake. It had to be. He was in there after Denton.

Hook was debating whether or not to go in when he heard a fusilade of muffled shots coming from the balcony—or Denton's apartment. When the firing ceased, Hook pushed through the batwings and moved cautiously across the floor, then started up the stairs. He was halfway up the flight when he heard more shots, and knew for sure this time that they came from Denton's apartment.

Cautiously, taking each step as if it might be his last, he eased himself up the stairs and then darted across the balcony. The door to Denton's apartment was closed. He nudged it open and peered down the narrow hallway just as he heard one thunderous, curiously muffled gunshot that seemed to come from Denton's office.

He ducked back out onto the balcony and waited for a good thirty seconds or more before reentering the apartment. Peering down the darkened hallway, he saw nothing to indicate trouble. He started down it. Only when he came upon the door leading into the living room did he notice the holes in the door and in the plaster on the wall opposite. Warily now, his rifle poking into the darkness ahead of him, he slipped silently on down the hallway until he was near the office doorway.

He paused, his head tipped, his mouth open slightly, as he listened for any sound coming from the office. He heard nothing. If a man was crouched in there, waiting, Hook would have been able to hear his breathing. But no one was alive inside that office. He was certain of it.

He stepped into the office and stumbled awkwardly when his feet got tangled in the two bodies sprawled on the floor. He placed his rifle down on top of Denton's desk, struck a match and lit the lamp sitting on the corner of it, then held it over his head so he could inspect the two dead men.

He recognized Pablo Sanchez at once. He had done a great job on Denton, blowing the back of his head out with a huge Walker Colt. Hook had been wrong. It was not Drake who had come after Denton, but Frank Ellison's foreman, avenging his boss's death.

Which meant Drake had other fish to fry. And maybe Hook was that fish. That did it. The hell with this place. Without Denton to back him, Hook was in trouble and had enough sense to know it. The sooner he put this fool town behind him, the better.

Hook blew out the lamp and hurried out of the apartment, anxious to reach his room and retrieve his money belt. He had already saddled his horse, his blanket roll and saddlebags tied on and ready, a precaution he was now well satisfied with himself for having taken.

Longarm left Hook's room only mildly discouraged. It did not look to him like the man had lit out yet. He was still around. Somewhere. As he entered the alley beside the barbershop he heard gunfire coming from the alley back of the express warehouse.

Drawing his Colt, he started toward the sound of the gunfire when he saw Slade, staggering from a wound, come boiling out of a side alley. He appeared to be attempting to make it to the Silverado. A second later, Tomlinson appeared, lugging his rifle. He too had apparently been wounded, and as Longarm watched, he saw Tomlinson collapse.

Glancing back, Slade saw Tomlinson's condition and came to a shambling halt, turned and staggered back, his six-gun out and pointing down at the fallen man. Longarm swung up his Colt and fired in one single motion. Slade was hit, the round forcing him to his knees, but he turned and flung up his rifle. A shot from the downed Tomlinson caught him between the shoulder blades, and Slade tumbled forward to the ground, dead.

Longarm hurried over to Tomlinson. "How bad are you hurt?"

"I ain't sure. But it hurts, and to tell you the truth, Drake, I'm getting pretty damn sick of this."

Looking past Longarm, Tomlinson's eyes widened in alarm. Longarm glanced over his shoulder. Hook, evidently drawn by the gunfire, was walking toward them, his rifle trained on them both, a grim smile on his face.

"You shoot us in plain sight like this, it'll be murder, Hook," Tomlinson said.

"Who's noticing?"

"I am!"

The three of them turned to see Jane stepping out of the alley her father and Slade had left a moment before. Her carbine was leveled on Hook as she moved closer. There seemed no doubt in Hook's mind that she knew how to use the weapon, and would, in defense of her father.

Still, Hook had not come this far without taking a few reckless gambles. Longarm saw the man's lean body tensing and knew he was about to start levering shots at Jane. Longarm still had his Colt in his hand and fired from his hip. The rifle in Hook's hand went flying.

The man cried out from the damage done to his hand, turned, and bolted across the street. As he neared the alley, Longarm stood up and snapped off another shot, but Hook did not slow and a second later vanished into the alley.

Jane came running. "Dad!" she cried.

"Hi, Jane. Glad you happened by when you did. That Hook was fixing to blow me and Drake into the next world."

"How bad is it?" she cried, unbuttoning his bloodied shirt.

"I ain't hurt all that bad," the old man grumbled, managing to eke out a smile as he patted Jane's hand. "Hell, I'm just gettin' used to it. But I'd sure appreciate it if you'd go get the doc."

"I'll get him, Jane," said Longarm. "You stay here with your father."

"He's probably in his office next to the church," she

told him. "That's where he took Jimmy. Jimmy's been wounded, too."

"Looks like we aren't doing so good."

"Yes, we are! The Kid's dead, and so is Slade."

In no mood to argue the point, Longarm stood up and looked around. Where was Hook? The abrupt clatter of hooves behind the barbershop told him. Hook was on his way out of there—and at that moment Longarm's bonus looked a long way off.

He turned and hurried down the street to get the doctor for Tomlinson.

Chapter 12

Longarm napped fitfully until an hour or so before dawn, and by the time light was showing in the east, he was riding out of town after Hook on Jane's chestnut, trailing a large, powerful roan. There was little difficulty finding Hook's tracks, and soon enough he became as familiar with them as with those left by his own horse.

He didn't follow Hook's trail directly. Once he had ascertained the direction he was taking, he circled wide of his route, aware that Hook would be watching his back trail, alert for pursuit. Longarm wasn't worried. He figured he had the edge. The man in black had to be weak still from his earlier loss of blood, he had taken a slug in his right hand, and he had been riding hard through the night.

Longarm pushed the chestnut to its limit, and when it

was close to the end of its tether, he dismounted, transferred his saddle to the roan, and rode off, leaving the lathered chestnut hobbled in a grassy, spring-fed meadow. He pushed the roan just as hard as he had the chestnut until a little before the noon hour when he found some high ground, a crumbling mesa. Dismounting, he climbed to the top of it and began sweeping the horizon south of him with a pair of binoculars.

An hour passed, however, before Longarm caught sight of Hook. Focusing the glasses, he saw that Hook was not pushing his horse, but letting it set its own pace. He rode well, sitting forward loosely to ease the horse's load. His right hand was thrust inside his frock coat, his left hand holding the reins. After Longarm's shot, Hook was now left-handed.

A man of Hook's skill and reputation, however, would not necessarily be at much of a disadvantage in a firefight. Hook could probably shoot as well with his left hand as he could with his right.

Longarm swept the glasses north. Ahead of Hook's trail were timbered foothills folding down toward a single, steep-sided pass. Longarm turned and scrambled back down behind the mesa, mounted the roan, and headed for the foothills, careful to keep the mesa between himself and Hook.

Hook had seen the glint of sunlight on glass and had known he was being tracked. He knew also that the pass he was approaching would be an ideal place for a bushwhacker to make his move. Who that bushwhacker might be, Hook had not the slightest doubt. Drake. Jud Drake. And before Hook killed the son of a bitch, he would find out what this was all about. A gambler interested in purchasing a hotel he was not.

The news brought in by a Circle D rider, that someone was changing the brands on Circle D stock and that Ellison was accusing Denton, was what had brought Hook out there to finish off the cripple. There was no doubt in Hook's mind now that Drake was behind the doctored brands. The more he thought about it, the more he realized that this fellow Drake had been nothin' less than a stick of dynamite set to go off in the middle of Denton's enterprises, blowing everyone and everything to hell and gone.

Fortunately, once he cleared Drake out of his path, it would be clear sailing. But even as he told himself this, he was aware that it did not make him feel any less apprehensive. This man Drake worried him. No question about it. Up until now Hook had seriously underestimated him, and as he felt the money belt pressing snugly against his waist, he told himself it would be decidedly unsafe for him to do so again.

Once into the pass, Hook guided his horse in under a rock shelf, and armed with the heavy, bolt-action rifle he had stolen from the barber, he started up the pass's southern slope, heading for the rimrocks high above the pass. It was more likely Drake was waiting for him on this slope, he figured. When Drake left that mesa, he would have been careful to keep it between Hook and him to avoid detection. And that would put Drake waiting on the slope south of the pass.

It took Hook a long while to reach the rimrocks, since he was more intent on moving quietly than on moving quickly. When he reached the cover of the rocks finally, he found himself with a fine view of the timbered slopes below and the floor of the pass beyond. Somewhere down in that timber, he knew, Drake was waiting.

Slowly, carefully, his keen eyes bright with concentration, he scanned the ground below him. He wished he had the glasses Drake had used to spot him, but it was no matter. At last he caught movement well off to his right, near the lip of a jutting ledge, a spot from which anyone with a rifle would have a clear shot at a rider moving through the pass. He smiled and waited so as to make sure and caught another movement, or rather, a shift of dark color between screening trees. Carrying the rifle in his left hand as easily as he would have a side arm, he left the rocks and started down the slope, angling to his right as he headed for the ledge.

He had not gone far before he glimpsed through the trees the shoulders of a man lying prone on the ledge, his rifle beside him. He smiled and kept going.

Longarm knew Hook was onto him when horse and rider failed to come out from under the rock face and continue on through the pass. He didn't have to know any more than that to realize that he must have given himself away somehow, and realized ruefully then that sunlight might have been reflected off his binoculars. The hell with it. If Hook knew he was up here somewhere, so much the better. All Longarm would have to do was wait for him to make his move.

Longarm waited a considerable time, listening, looking—and finally caught a glimpse of the man well up the slope behind him moving steadily toward the rimrocks.

That gave Longarm two options.

172

He could go up there after him, conceding Hook the high ground. Or he could trick Hook into coming down here after him.

He chose the second course and decided he would have to give the man a target, something to act as a lure. Remembering a ledge farther along he had decided against using because it was too exposed, he slipped back to it, laid his coat down onto it close by screening trees, put his rifle alongside it, then moved back into the pines screening the ridge, and with his eyes peering up at the slope, waited.

When close to half an hour passed and there was no sign that Hook had caught sight of his lure, he began moving back and forth in the trees flanking the ledge. He didn't do it for long, just long enough to catch Hook's eye. If Hook did not bite soon, Longarm realized grimly, he would just have to go up after him.

The first indication that Longarm's ruse had worked was the sound of dislodged pebbles on the slope to Longarm's left. His Colt out, Longarm kept low, and waited. Hook made no more mistakes, and with a suddenness that was startling, he appeared in plain sight just behind the ledge. The moment he saw the frock coat laid out on the ledge, the rifle alongside it, he realized he had walked into a trap and spun quickly about, looking for Longarm.

Longarm had a clear shot through the trees; he aimed and fired. But Hook was ducking aside even as Longarm squeezed the trigger. The round snipped off a low-hanging branch. Hook blasted at Longarm through the trees, missing Longarm, but not by much. Longarm charged out of the cover, his Colt blazing, but Hook stood his ground, seemingly unscathed, and Longarm saw that his rifle was a single-shot, bolt-action.

Pulling up, he flung up his Colt to finish Hook off.

Swinging the rifle like a cue stick, Hook slammed Longarm's Colt out of his hand, the heavy barrel finishing up in Longarm's gut. Longarm went down on one knee, but managed to grab the rifle's barrel with both hands and wrest it out of Hook's grasp. As he lurched back with the rifle, Hook put his head down and charged, bowling Longarm back. He felt his boots scraping on the ledge, and then there was nothing under his feet as he toppled into space.

About twenty feet below the ledge he came down hard on the face of a boulder, the impact momentarily knocking the breath out of him. Blinking up at the sky, Longarm saw Hook step into view on the ledge above him. He was a mess. Evidently not all of Longarm's shots had gone wild. In addition to his bloody right hand, there were growing bloodstains high on his shirt-front. But the man was holding the rifle in the crook of his right arm and was slowly, carefully, pulling back the bolt with his left hand. Then he shifted the rifle into his left hand and, aiming it like a handgun, sighted on Longarm.

Longarm kicked his feet and rolled off the boulder, coming to rest on the ground between it and a smaller boulder close by. The space was narrow and Longarm was jammed in between them for a moment. Calmly shifting his aim, Hook fired. The round seared the flesh between Longarm's chest and his forearm before pounding harmlessly into the pine needles. Longarm saw his chance and, crying out, flung himself over and began to twist like one who had sustained a painful wound.

As he did so, he palmed the derringer from his fob pocket.

He continued to moan and twist slowly as Hook climbed down with great difficulty beside him. Longarm felt the man's shadow looming over him, saw his boot a moment before he buried it into Longarm's side and rolled him over. Hook had a knife in his hand and raised it over his head, preparing to bury the blade into Longarm's chest.

Hook blinked in surprise as he found himself peering into the twin bores of the tiny derringer in Longarm's fist. With a fatalistic calm, he lifted the knife still higher over his head. Longarm emptied both barrels into a spot under the man's chin, the two rounds ranging up through his skull and exploding out through its top.

Hook was a dead man even before the knife dropped from his nerveless fingers.

What awakened Longarm was the pounding of the carpenters' hammers as they continued to work on the line's new barn. Or that's what he thought until the knock came on his door again.

He sat up. "Who is it?"

"Jane!"

"I'm not decent."

"You're always decent."

With a sigh, Longarm threw off the covers, draped one of the sheets over his naked frame, and padded over to the door. Unlocking it, he pulled it open. Jane entered, smiling.

"You look like a Roman senator," she told him as he closed the door.

"How would you know what a Roman senator looked like?"

"I'll tell you all about that someday."

Scratching his head, Longarm moved back to his bed and sat down on the edge of it. "What's up?" he asked.

"That's what I should be asking you," she retorted.

Sitting down on the edge of his bed, she proceeded to take off her boots, her shirt, and then finally her Levi's. There was nothing left after that to remove. He watched in mild astonishment as she crawled under his covers.

With a shrug, he joined her. She was right. He was up.

Afterward, she lay with her cheek on his bare chest, her finger tracing a line from his neck to his thigh, teasingly.

"The barn's coming along fine," she said. "This time we'll have nearly twice the space, for all those horses we're buying."

"You can use them."

"That was generous of you, Jud. I never really expected you to invest all that money."

"You thought I was a four-flusher."

"Never mind what I thought." Her hot little hand was resting on the best part of him. "The truth is, you are a strange, mysterious man."

"I have a confession to make."

"I'm listening."

"That money I invested wasn't my own."

She propped herself up on her elbow and looked at him in astonishment. "Why, whatever do you mean?"

She drew her educated finger away from his crotch and he wished she hadn't.

"It was donated by Bull Denton through the offices of James B. Hook."

"I don't understand."

He explained about the money belt he had found on Hook's corpse. And where it must have come from, and why.

She sighed, troubled obviously by this disclosure. "That was Hook's payoff for killing Ellison, then."

"That's the way I figure it."

"Then you *are* a four-flusher. You never had money of your own to invest."

"Does it matter?"

"Of course not."

She kissed him, and let her hand drop back to where it was doing him so much good. He closed his eyes and leaned back.

"But I was thinking," she continued after a minute. "Ellison's housekeeper, that Zuni Indian woman, stopped into the express office yesterday. She had her two kids with her and was looking for a job. She has no rights to Ellison's holdings, of course. She wasn't even legally married to him."

"Too bad."

"I felt very sorry for her. Maybe she could work for the line. She's very intelligent. Her kids could work as stable hands, and she'd do fine in the office."

Longarm kissed her on the lips. "Not a bad idea."

"And since that money was Hook's reward for killing Ellison, I might even make her a partner," Jane said eagerly, her eyes brightening at the prospect. "She'd never have to know anything about the money or where it came from."

Laughing with delight at the thought, she dropped her lips to his and used her tongue to great effect. A moment before, he was convinced he was spent, utterly —but here he was ready for her again. He looked past her at the block of sunlight on the ceiling. It seemed to fill the room with a golden light.

Then she moved her head and he couldn't see the ceiling as her long chestnut curls fell over his face, her mouth still covering his, her fingers lighting a fire in his crotch. He closed his eyes, and with a delighted laugh, she lowered herself onto him and he grabbed her hips in his big hands and rolled himself over onto her and began it all over again.

He tried to forget he was not Jud Drake and that she could never be allowed to know him for the man he really was. If he wasn't a four-flusher, he sure as hell was an imposter. And then he managed to forget what that meant and all the rest of it, and there was only this bright, golden morning and the passionate heat of this woman beneath him.

A woman he would be leaving behind before this day was out.

Billy Vail had draped an arm over his shoulder when he handed Longarm his bonus. A bank draft for five hundred dollars. It was a considerable sum, and Billy had suggested for the second time that Longarm would be wise to invest it in that widow's ranch outside Denver. Longarm had said nothing at the time, but he had decided to give it serious consideration, and was now on the way out to Helen Goodnight's ranch to accept the pretty widow's long-standing proposition.

He had managed to save most of the five hundred he had started out with, giving him close to eight hundred silver dollars resting now in his saddlebags, and all during this ride out to the Lazy G, he had been getting himself used to the idea of becoming Helen's business partner.

And all that went with it.

Having started out before dawn, he rode into the ranch's compound a little before noon. He pulled up in front of the big white house and dismounted. He waved to a few of the hands moving about the compound, dropped his reins over the hitch rail, and was halfway up the porch steps when a tall, rugged-looking man in his early thirties with shoulders as wide as a barn door strode out onto the porch.

"Howdy, stranger," he said to Longarm. "You're welcome to light a spell. What's your business?"

Longarm wasn't sure how to answer that and held up in some confusion. He was saved when Helen burst out onto the porch, arms wide, a broad smile on her face.

"Custis!" she cried. "What a lovely surprise!"

"In the neighborhood," he said. "Just thought I'd drop in."

"I would never have forgiven you if you hadn't."

She hurried quickly over to him and, taking his hand in hers, led him up the stairs onto the porch, still beaming.

"Hank," she said to the lean, rawboned man beside her. "This here is my very good friend, Custis Long. He's a United States deputy marshal."

The man shook Longarm's hand with a solid, un-

compromising grip. It was clear he didn't like Longarm
—that is, he didn't like the way Longarm had just ridden in and started up the steps.

"Hank," Helen cried, "be a dear and go tell Cookie
we're having a guest for dinner."

Hank did not hesitate, and as he ambled off the
porch, heading for the cookshack, Helen beamed at
Longarm. "Isn't he handsome! He rode in two weeks
ago, looking for a job as foreman. Of course, I hired
him right off."

"How's he doin'?"

"Oh, my, Custis. I don't think there's a horse he
can't break or a man he can't beat. And of course he can
tame me any time he wants."

"He's working out then."

"Magnificently."

Longarm turned and descended the porch steps. After
he had stepped into his saddle, he touched the brim of
his hat to her. "Thanks for the invite, but I got to be
pushin' on."

"Must you?"

"Yes, I really must. And thank you."

"But Custis, thank me for what."

"Next time you come into Denver, look me up. I'll
tell you then."

He hauled his horse around. Touching his heels
lightly to its flanks, he lifted the animal to a canter.

As he rode out through the gate, he was chuckling in
relief. He had been perfectly serious in thanking Helen,
and sure as hell grateful for the lesson. He figured
maybe it was him thinking of Jane and that stage line
that led him to consider joining up with Helen. Well, he
was cured now, and a damn sight richer than he would

have been if he hadn't been introduced to that tall, raw-boned foreman who could break any horse and tame any woman.

He leaned back in his saddle and relaxed, looking forward eagerly to the Windsor Hotel that night, and to a fine sporting game of poker. He might double his fortune or lose it all on the flip of a card, and there'd be no one who could deny him the right to take that chance.

Watch for

**LONGARM AND THE TREACHEROUS
TRIAL**

one hundred seventeenth in the bold
LONGARM series from Jove

coming in September!